Your Wellness Toolbox

Your Wellness Toolbox

Ali Swift

Author photograph by Hannah Martinig Photography

Matador
9 Priory Business Park,
Wistow Road, Kibworth Beauchamp,
Leicestershire. LE8 0RX
Tel: 0116 279 2299
Email: books@troubador.co.uk
Web: www.troubador.co.uk/matador
Twitter: @matadorbooks

ISBN 978 1800461 185

British Library Cataloguing in Publication Data.
A catalogue record for this book is available from the British Library.

Printed and bound in Great Britain by 4edge Limited
Typeset in 11pt Minion Pro by Troubador Publishing Ltd, Leicester, UK

Matador is an imprint of Troubador Publishing Ltd

Swifty, Thomas & Elouise
The love, light and laughter in my every day.
My World.
Thank You.

CONTENTS

YOUR TOOLS

YOUR SCENARIOS

YOUR WELLNESS TOOLBOX CHALLENGES

YOUR WELLNESS TOOLBOX

In August 2006, following eight years(ish) of struggling with anxiety and panic attacks, I hit rock bottom; within weeks I was sitting in a talking therapy session and I was introduced to My Wellness Toolbox.

I started to fill it with the tools that helped me let go of trauma from the past, to help me rebuild my self-esteem, that taught me how to love myself and that made me feel happy again. That made me grab life by the balls once more and live a more positive life.

Over the years I have continued to discover new tools as I navigated my way through both the exciting and heartbreaking challenges of life and anything and everything that could be a trigger for the crippling anxiety or depression taking over once more. 'It' has tried several times, more recently in 2019; more on this later.

As the tools in My Wellness Toolbox have saved me so many times, I whipped out Tool #25, started writing at the end of 2017, and by August 2018 *My Wellness Toolbox* was published, sharing with you 26 of the incredible tools that helped me. I wanted to encourage you to discover *Your* Wellness Toolbox and fill it with the tools that work for *you*, to either overcome mental health challenges or to simply live a more positive life.

The release of *My Wellness Toolbox* led me to talk tools more publicly. The more I talked to *you* via events, workshops, radio and 121 coaching sessions about *Your* Wellness Toolbox and y*our* power tools I realised how much *you* were also helping me, how *you* were adding new tools to *My* Wellness Toolbox.

Your life experiences, *your* coping strategies, *your* tools have led me to add 14 more tools to My Wellness Toolbox.

In *Your Wellness Toolbox* I will be sharing the extra tools, giving more practical tips on how to use the tools in different scenarios, and there may be a challenge or ten, encouraging you to proactively use *Your* Wellness Toolbox.

I am not a doctor, psychotherapist, psychologist, or medical specialist of any kind, I would never claim to be. I am just a young woman who found a way to manage and overcome anxiety and depression. I want to share the tools that helped me and that are still working for me today.

Are you ready to discover new tools for Your Wellness Toolbox?

GETTING STARTED

If you have not yet discovered or started using Your Wellness Toolbox here are my four key tips to get started:

1. Keep It Simple

Start off by writing a list of *positive* coping mechanisms you already use in your daily routine and/or activities you enjoy that calm or uplift you.

For example:

- Music – I always turn on my positive playlist on my way to the office, especially when I have a busy day ahead.
- No media – I do not watch the news or read newspapers when going through stressful periods and challenging times.

- Exercise – I love walking and talking; a good natter with a friend is always guaranteed to make us both feel better.
- Writing – I enjoy writing and try to write in my journal at least twice a week.
- Massage – a good massage therapy always uplifts me.

2. Visualise Your Tools in Your Wellness Toolbox

Acknowledge that everything on your list is one of your tools and place them visually in Your Wellness Toolbox.

3. Use Your Tools Proactively

Now you have acknowledged these are the tools that help and support you, use them and be grateful for them.

Do not just use your tools during the challenging times to make you feel better, also use them proactively with the aim of heading into the challenging times more positively.

4. Share and Discover New Tools

As you go through your everyday seek out new tools that make you feel good, boost your confidence and encourage a positive mind. It is when you share your tools with others that you may just discover new power tools.

MY WELLNESS TOOLBOX

Tools 1–26 are the original tools I shared in My Wellness Toolbox. Tools 27–40 are the tools I have discovered since that book was published (or the ones I forgot to include!). How many of them are in Your Wellness Toolbox?

1. WATER ☐
2. BREATHE ☐
3. MUSIC ☐
4. MEDIA – TURN IT OFF ☐
5. ESSENTIAL OILS ☐
6. COGNITIVE BEHAVIOURAL THERAPY ☐
7. GRATITUDE VISION BOARD ☐
8. RESCUE REMEDY ☐
9. DAILY SELF-CARE ☐
10. ACCEPTANCE ☐
11. AFFIRMATIONS ☐
12. NO ☐
13. SELF-HELP BOOKS ☐
14. POSITIVE PEOPLE ☐
15. GRATITUDE ☐
16. LET GO & RELEASE TECHNIQUES ☐
17. REIKI ☐

18. *THE SECRET, THE POWER, THE MAGIC* ☐
19. MASSAGE THERAPIES ☐
20. LEARN SOMETHING NEW ☐
21. KINDNESS ☐
22. PHYSICAL EXERCISE ☐
23. LAUGHTER ☐
24. HYPNOBIRTHING ☐
25. WRITING ☐
26. ME (YOU) ☐
27. TALKING ☐
28. CRYING ☐
29. HUGGING ☐
30. THE BEACH ☐
31. SUNSETS ☐
32. GUIDED MEDITATION ☐
33. YES ☐
34. CRYSTALS ☐
35. TEACHING OTHERS ☐
36. DRAWING ☐
37. DECLUTTERING ☐
38. PLACENTA ENCAPSULATION ☐
39. FORGIVENESS ☐
40. YOU (THAT'S ME!) ☐

Just take the tools from My Wellness Toolbox that help you and ignore the tools that just do not work for you. There are no right or wrong tools (unless of course your tools involve breaking the law – probably best to avoid these).

What works for you is what is right for you.

YOUR WELLNESS
TOOLBOX?

Before you go any further list the tools in Your Wellness
Toolbox below...

1.

2.

3.

4.

5.

6.

7.

8.

9.

10.

11.

12.

13.

14.

15.

16.

17.

18.

19.

20.

21.

22.

23.

24.

25.

… Continue to add your tools as you discover them.

TALKING TOOLS BLOG
"I'M (STILL) NOT OK RIGHT NOW AND THAT'S OK!"
1 October 2019

Although I am honest in all the Talking Tools blogs, I acknowledge that most of them are light-hearted and may only reflect the positive outcomes I have when I use my tools. This is intentional as I try to plant seeds and encourage you to explore my tools to help you discover your tools, and positivity breeds positivity. I try to steer clear of the negative posts that may trigger you.

Today I have chosen to go a little deeper as I feel it is important to share that even this Reiki therapist, wellness coach and author of a wellness book is not immune from mental health issues returning to slap me in the face. I considered doing a 'live' but I'm just too tired to talk, it will end in tears and I have a feeling pulling out Tool #25 may help me (and hopefully one or more of you) today.

For those of you who have watched the recent 'lives' you will know that for several months anxiety has been creeping back into my life and my tools have been used more in the past six months than in the last 13 years, mostly with success. However, it still led me to visit the doctor in July as my instinct, mixed with brittle nails, breaking hair and spotty skin, was telling me something was not quite right (the body really is amazing at sending us messages). After a blood test and a phone call to the doctor a few days later, it was confirmed over the phone that I had a B12 deficiency (again). *That's OK*, I thought, *at least I now know; that can be sorted easily.* I had a B12 deficiency when my eldest was a few months old. The doctor prescribed B12 supplements; they made a positive difference within two weeks! I tried to book a routine appointment to see the doctor to discuss further, however I was unable to get an appointment before I was going away for four weeks. Therefore, I popped to the health food shop and picked up some B12 supplements… and until yesterday have been taking one a day (well, most days).

In the past two weeks the anxiety has really ramped up. Whilst exciting news and opportunities were flying at me from all directions, I was becoming more overwhelmed and less excited, even demotivated. This is not the 'normal' me. By the time I flew out to work with my dad in Dublin last Tuesday anxiety levels were the highest they have been in 13 years, my tools working overtime. I actually felt a bit scared. I nearly did not get on the plane. It was the massage chair... water... Rescue Remedy... affirmations... Reiki... gratitude... *me* (!) that helped calm me down (and my newfound love of puzzle books), but by the time I got off the plane and was greeted by my dad I was smiling but felt exhausted.

The next few days Dad and I really enjoyed working together as we designed some great Your Workplace Wellness workshops and I was able to spend some quality time with my 90-year-old grandparents. I had a good time, yet I constantly felt anxiety was always hanging around waiting to greet me on the next corner. I struggled to eat in the mornings, felt overwhelmed as I brainstormed new ideas, anxious as we went into new places and tearful at the thought I was spiralling back down into a dark hole that I have not seen for 13 years (and have no intentions of revisiting). Overthinking sucks.

I spoke to my dad and was honest about how I was feeling (most of the time). He agreed that another visit to the doctor was a must and not a should... and that Dr Google was not the way forward (old habits pop up = slapped wrists) as that was just adding to the confusion, overthinking and tiredness.

Then I landed home on Friday and the weekend happened. Friday evening ended with me in tears spilling all my frustrations and feelings over my extremely understanding husband who has never really seen this side of me – a massive release. Yet when I woke up on Saturday,

I have never felt so tired (and I have two small children). I spent most of Saturday and Sunday napping, sleeping, yawning or trying to convince the family to snuggle on the sofa and watch movies. I did not go outside once (and I love fresh air). I have also been feeling extremely low, tearful and not myself. So frustrating as I have no obvious reasons to feel like this. Life is great right now, so why am I not feeling like it is? As a dollop of guilt lands on my head... ouch!

So yesterday morning I called the doctor once more and managed to book an appointment. A few hours later I am sat in front of the doctor, sharing with him the latest list of 'symptoms' hoping this may help. Following an initial discussion, he asked what I was taking for the B12 deficiency. I proudly presented my high-quality (and expensive) pot of B12 supplements. The doctor quickly advised that unfortunately they would not have really made any difference to my B12 levels as the dosage is significantly less than what I require! Doh!! So, it looks like my body has been ringing the alarm bells and screaming at me to return to the doctor. I'm so glad I finally listened. I have now been prescribed a course of five B12 injections over the next two weeks. They started yesterday. I have everything crossed that these will help.

Today I have been on an emotional rollercoaster. Obviously, the injections will not work overnight so I am still extremely tired, which appears to be best buddies with anxiety, headaches and overthinking at the moment. I have pulled out Tool #17 – Reiki (thanks to the lovely Jaki Bourne), which took the edge off and has calmed me down, pulled out Tool #9 – Daily Self-Care, and rearranged all my appointments and meetings for the week ahead so I can have some downtime. At first, I felt a bit guilty doing this but quickly realised my body is telling me I need to give me a break so I can be the mummy my kids need me to be and have the positive energy my clients need me to have. I also picked up the phone and spoke to one of my Tool #14s, my best friend. Talking really does help release the anxiety; she was amazing.

Tool #11 – Affirmations – "This too will pass" and "I have a healthy mind and a healthy body" – are also on repeat right now.

I have definitely learned a lesson the hard way. I knew that the anxiety that was creeping back in was different to 13 years ago; this was not the result of Post-Traumatic Stress Disorder (PTSD). Therefore, self-prescribing supplements for a deficiency is really not a good idea (*slapped wrists once more*). Even if you can't make the follow-up appointment following a blood test try and seek advice from your GP over the phone (and not just a chat with the surgery receptionist). I have had to pull out the acceptance tool to forgive myself on this one. Next step is to pull out the 'let go and release' techniques so I can move forward more positively from the last few weeks and not get caught up in the negative thinking; this will only suck me into the black hole.

My Wellness Toolbox has always been invaluable in recent months and I feel so lucky to have the tools with me. As I continue to discover new ones they are getting added straight away.

I need to be clear that I have not shared this for sympathy, a telling-off or applause. I have simply shared to help the one person with whom this may resonate, to encourage them to ask for help, discourage them from self-diagnosing, definitely discourage them from self-prescribing, to encourage them not to assume this is "the same as last time" and maybe to help them discover a tool or two for their Wellness Toolbox.

I know it sucks, yet it is OK not to feel OK, but it is not OK to let yourself struggle in silence. Please ask for help.

PS. Writing this has helped me a little! I love Tool #25! Give it a go.

TOOL #27
TALKING

It was only when I started Talking Tools and sharing my mental health experiences at events and workshops that it really started to sink in how important 'talking' is; it is also contagious. Talking about how you are feeling or what you have experienced encourages others to do the same.

Studies have proven that simply talking about our problems and sharing our negative emotions with someone can be profoundly healing; it can reduce stress, strengthen our immune system, and can also reduce physical and emotional distress.

Tool #6 – Cognitive Behavioural Therapy, a talking therapy, is already in My Wellness Toolbox, yet I feel 'talking' should be a tool in its own right. So, in it goes. I now consider it one of my most critical tools; it can save lives.

About nine months after *My Wellness Toolbox* was released, life became very busy – exciting times but busy times. I was juggling far too many things, including three jobs, my family and social life. I was not using Tool #9 – Daily Self-Care effectively, I was not using Tool #12 – NO enough, and then a wonderful family friend tragically passed away and I found it very hard to accept, especially the pain it was causing his family.

By July 2019 for the first time in years I started to experience daily anxiety and panic attacks again. Although 'it' had kindly thrown me a few warning signs, 'it' spiralled very quickly. I was waking up most days with those exam-day knots in my stomach and adrenaline rushes that made me feel as though I had just fallen off a theme park ride, and I was worrying about anything and everything. I was scared. I was scared by my own thoughts and scared that I was losing control. I was also scared to talk about it.

Fortunately, my history reminded me not to make the same mistake again. This time I was not going to deal with 'it' in my own head for eight years and wait for rock bottom to find me, so I talked. I talked to my dad. I talked to my mum. I talked to my sister. I talked to my close friends. I talked to the positive people in my life. I was open and honest about how I was feeling. Talking somehow took the pressure off. It really did help.

Most importantly I talked to my husband. I was extremely open and honest with him, as scary as it felt at the time. I talked to him about my feelings and things that have happened in my life that I have never told anyone. He talked back. He did not understand it all but as he pointed out, he did not need to, I just needed to know I could talk to him. I think he sometimes wishes I would stop!

He also encouraged me to seek professional help.

A visit to the GP and a blood test later it was confirmed (as I had expected) I had a B12 deficiency once more. This explained so many things, including the anxiety, depressive thoughts, weak nails, poor skin, hair breakage. However, to cut a long and quite boring story short I was unable to see a doctor to discuss my results, so I naively made a few assumptions and prescribed myself (with the help of a lovely health shop assistant) some good quality B12 supplements. It would be another ten weeks before I sat in front of another GP, my mental health significantly deteriorating at this point, to be told I would need B12 injections; the self-prescribed supplements would not have helped in any way (I had such an urge to slap myself). I would later be diagnosed with pernicious anaemia (I still cannot pronounce it), which means my body has an inability to absorb the essential vitamin B12 that is needed for your body to make enough healthy red blood cells. That explains the fatigue.

B12 injections made a significant improvement very quickly; the brain fog, headaches and fatigue disappeared within weeks. However, anxiety had made itself quite comfortable and the negative mindset also had its feet firmly under the table. A B12 injection was not going to be enough. Talking to the rescue once more.

It took another couple of months and the advice of an incredibly supportive Tool #14 – Positive Person in my life to realise that although talking to friends and family was the right thing to be doing, it was possibly not enough, and I should talk to a professional.

In November 2019 I found myself pulling out Tool #6 and was sat in a therapist's chair once more, talking.

Talking about how I really feel about things from my past and present and any worries I may have about the future. The therapist then worked with me to change patterns of behaviour that are not helpful for me. It was effective very quickly and by Christmas 2019 I was feeling a lot more positive, anxiety had significantly reduced, and I felt all my other tools had been recharged also. I have decided that this tool is one that I should try and use proactively when I can afford to. Therefore, going forward I plan to have regular talking therapy top-ups as it has been very effective for me.

Talking about how we feel is so important. Please do it. Do not stop doing it. Never feel like a burden. Talking can also help others.

If you are reading this and feel you need to talk but do not feel you have someone you can trust to talk to, or for some reason you feel like a burden, there are a number of national helplines that can help you. These can be found with a quick internet search.

Just talk.

Effectiveness: 10/10. Just talk.

Ease: 5/10. It is not easy, it is one of the hardest tools to use in My Wellness Toolbox, yet sometimes the hardest things to do bring us exactly what we need.

Cost: Free – £150. It shouldn't cost anything to talk to a loved one. Talking to a professional normally comes with a charge. This ranges across the country, between £40 and £150 per hour.

"There are many ways of getting strong, sometimes talking is the best way."

(Andre Agassi)

JUST FEELING
A BIT FED UP?

My Wellness Toolbox does not just help me proactively when I am facing situations that have historically made me feel anxious. I often call upon them in everyday scenarios to give me a boost when needed.

Yesterday morning I woke up feeling really run down and full of cold; I knew that I needed to boost both energy and positivity, and quickly. Not just for my sake but for the little Swifts too. No one needs cranky Mummy, especially when Daddy is working away.

The lid was lifted, the tools started flying at me; I continued to catch them until bedtime.

TOOL #1 WATER

When feeling under the weather this tool always remains loyal by my side, keeping me hydrated and clearing the brain fog. I also sipped on hot water and lemon several times throughout the day; this was both warming and soothing.

TOOL #5 ESSENTIAL OILS

The diffuser went straight on. I internet-searched 'essential oils for stuffy head and nose' and came across this lovely blend:

- 3 drops peppermint
- 1 drop lavender
- 1 drop eucalyptus
- 1 drop wild orange (I'm not sure how 'wild' my orange is – but in it went)

Then when the children were tucked up in bed, I put all the paperwork and washing piles to one side. I ran a hot bath and in went a few drops of my Women's Balance relaxing blend (Neal's Yard). I also added 1KG of Himalayan salts, not only great for the skin but can clear sinuses and induce relaxation. I melted for 30 minutes and got out feeling super relaxed.

TOOL #9 DAILY SELF-CARE

When I am feeling run down, I know this is my body reminding my mind to pull out one of my most valuable tools, Tool #9.

So, I didn't go without my morning hot shower, in fact I made sure the children were safely watching YouTube Kids on the tablets and stayed in for an extra few minutes.

I didn't cancel my weekly 'walk 'n' talk' planned with my good friend. My foggy head didn't want to face the cold, but as the sun was still shining, we soon warmed up as we chatted away, putting the weekend world to rights, our girls enjoying a Monday morning snooze in their pushchairs. This was also a wonderful use of Tools #14 – Positive People and #22 – Physical Exercise. I felt so much better by lunchtime.

I decided to have tea with the children, instead of grabbing something (no doubt convenient and unhealthy) later on. A bowl of chicken soup with a crusty bread roll put a big smile on my face (even if I was fighting off the children as apparently Mummy's food – even when the same – requires a full tasting).

I pulled out Tool #12 – NO and didn't pour a glass of wine from the half-full (very rare) bottle in the fridge.

I had a hot bath.

I had an early night. In bed by 8.30pm (never heard of in this house!)… and my head hit that pillow fast!! However, my mind and body must have been in shock as I was wide awake by midnight ready to get up and go!! This self-care plan had backfired on me as I then struggled to fall back to sleep wondering what every little sound was, which is why I then called upon Tool #17 (see below); another tool will always come to the rescue!!

TOOL #15 GRATITUDE

Even though I was feeling run down and didn't feel very thankful for it when my eyes first opened, I knew that I had to switch that mentality if I wanted to have a good day. That was my choice.

So, I said my three morning 'thank yous' as I got out of bed. This included:

- Thank you that my body is giving me the signals to look after myself.

… and by the end of the day:

- Thank you that my husband is working away so I can have a nice warm bath, early night and won't be disturbed by Xbox FIFA updates.

TOOL #17 REIKI

The amazing thing about Reiki is that if you are attuned at Level 1 you can use it for self-healing, so when I couldn't drop back off to sleep (and I had spent the best part of two hours tossing and turning) I pulled out this tool. I guess it was whilst using it that I fell asleep… and when I woke up this morning, I was ready to go!

Tool #3 – Music – of the relaxing variety – is a good alternative if you do not have Reiki readily available to you at 2am in the morning.

TOOL #26 ME (THAT'S YOU!)

I knew I wasn't on the right path when I woke up yesterday, so I charged up my tools, looked after *me* and today I feel so much better for it!!!

Talking Tools Blog: Originally published October 2019

YOUR GRATITUDE

Write Down Ten Things You Are Grateful For Today

1.

2.

3.

4.

5.

6.

7.

8.

9.

10.

You don't have to stop there...

TOOL #28
CRYING

Today my youngest didn't want to go into nursery; this is a rare occurrence, so it obviously raises the mummy guilt. I returned to my car and I burst into tears. The reality is that as soon as I drove off, she would be fine running around with her friends. I knew this. I questioned why I was crying, 'pulled myself together' and stopped.

I got home as my husband was leaving, said goodbye and as soon as I shut the door I started crying again. I questioned myself and quickly realised this was not because of the mummy guilt felt in the nursery car park but because my overthinking mind and body right now needs a good cry. It needs to release… and that's OK!!! Pulling myself together and holding back the tears is the wrong thing to do for my emotional wellbeing.

I am officially adding crying as a tool to My Wellness Toolbox. I now appreciate it can be very good for your wellbeing, especially during difficult times or when you are struggling with your mental health. It is OK to cry. Let's face it, we enter this world waving this tool in the air.

I have always worn my emotions on my sleeve. Until I wrote *My Wellness Toolbox*, I had an outdated belief that this was not a good thing, it was a sign of weakness. I have been told on a number of occasions that I shouldn't wear my heart or emotions on my sleeve so much (apparently it put boys off… but it didn't put the right one off!). This is who I am. Fortunately, I now have hard evidence that wearing my heart on my sleeve and sharing my emotions not only bagged me a great husband but has helped others, so I have since released that outdated belief.

However, I still get frustrated with myself that I cry for all different emotions and not just when I am sad. I am one of those that also cries when I am anxious, frustrated (this is the one that bugs me), angry (I think this one bugs my husband too), happy… and when I get the fit of giggles it can lead to full-on sobs!

When you see someone cry, how often is your reaction "Oh don't cry, it is going to be OK", "What are you crying for?", "Please stop crying, you'll upset me"?

What if crying is what they need to make them feel better?

How often do you hold back the tears and then start to experience additional anxiety, worry, stress or headaches?

What if crying is what you need to make you feel better?

I have done some research. It turns out tears are healthy, and crying can be very good for you. This is why:

- Crying can be uplifting – as we sob our breathing changes and also cools us down, which can actually help soothe our mind.
- Crying is self-soothing – crying activates the parasympathetic nervous system enabling your body to rest. It is not an immediate response but within minutes of crying the PNS will activate.
- Tears detox the body – research suggests that emotional tears contain stress hormones and when we cry, we are flushing them away (so that explains my recent weight loss).
- Crying releases endorphins including oxytocin – these are feel-good chemicals that can help relieve both emotional and physical pain. This happens when you have a good cry for a longer period of time.
- Crying rebalances you – when you experience a strong emotion crying helps rebalance your mind; this explains why I cry after a fit of giggles!!!
- Crying is important when grieving – releasing tears following the loss of a loved one is really important to help your mind process and accept what has happened.

Please, don't hold back those tears, release them as this is normal and healthy!

If you see someone holding back the tears, give them a big hug and let them know it is good to release them!

However, if you are crying excessively, you are worrying about how much you are crying and/or it is starting to interfere with your every day then I would suggest you have a chat with your GP to see if there are any underlying reasons that they can help you address.

When I started writing this blog my eyes were still stinging from the tears; they have since dried up and I am now feeling so much better than I did in the nursery car park two hours ago. This not only proves some of the above but also highlights that Tool #25 – Writing is once again working for me. What a combination!!

Effectiveness: 9/10. Crying works for me nine times out of ten; I think it does depend on the hormones.

Ease: 9/10. For me crying is easy when I let the tears go. Although once I pop, I struggle to stop.

Cost: Free. Crying does not cost a thing.

TOOL #29
HUGGING

We have talked (Tool #27), we have cried (Tool #28), so now let's hug it out.

Last night I was overthinking, overtired and overemotional; my husband recognised words were not going to help me in that moment. He came over and gave me a big hug that seemed to last for minutes; this actually resulted in me crying, but it was the release I needed, and it did make me feel better and the overthinking dissolved. Hugging is a tool that I need to call upon more often.

This is one for all the family. If you see someone who looks like they could do with a hug, they probably do, so step forward and give them one of your biggest hugs (obviously if they accept, could be pretty awkward otherwise). Always hold for at least 20 seconds for that extra charge of positivity and to help reduce the stress hormones.

… And if you are home alone and in need of a hug, it has been scientifically proven that hugging it out with a teddy can have the same health benefits as hugging it out with another human; it can reduce the stress levels and even soothe fears.

Effectiveness: 8/10. A good hug can really squeeze out the negativity.

Ease: 7/10. I love a good hug but even I can find it difficult to ask for one when I am really in need of one, especially if feeling low or grumpy. I do find it easier to give my hugs away than ask for one.

Cost: Free.

Talking Tools Blog – Originally published September 2019 (when hugging was not restricted by a Global Pandemic)

"A hug is always the right size."
(Winnie-the-Pooh)

YOUR DAILY
SELF-CARE ROUTINE

It is only when we take care of ourselves that we can effectively take care of others.

It is so easy to forget to care for the person that looks back at us in the mirror every day, yet caring for yourself is one of the most important things you can do for your physical self, your mind and your emotions, and when we take care of ourselves effectively we become more effective in all areas of our lives.

Write down all the things you
do every day for *you*:

If you need more than one page, that is brilliant, you clearly have the daily self-care tool in Your Wellness Toolbox.

If you have very little on your list, or nothing at all, or if your current daily self-care routine does not seem to be working for you, spend some time now thinking of the simple things you can introduce into your every day to uplift you, relax you, motivate you and build you. They do not have to be time-consuming and can cost very little or nothing at all.

A few examples of the things I do for me every day include: hot shower with invigorating shower gel to start the day; essential oils in the diffuser; positive playlist played throughout the day; lunch break; practising gratitude; bedtime meditation to help me sleep. All very simple yet all very positive for me.

The next step is to implement these self-care activities into your every day and then continue to do this exercise on a regular basis. You are worth it.

HOLIDAYS

Something many of us do every year for our self-care is book a holiday. Just the thought of a holiday once it is booked will make most people bounce around the room with excitement. A chance to relax or go on an adventure, a break from your everyday routine, bringing opportunities to experience new places, learn about different cultures and make amazing memories.

However, for several years the initial excitement of going on holiday once it was booked would easily turn to dread; even the sunniest of holidays would have the grey cloud of anxiety hovering over and panic would set in, normally as the bags were being packed. I can recall at least two occasions when I was physically sick at the airport as the nerves kicked in.

In 2011 when my boyfriend (now husband) and I booked our round the-world tickets I remember crying, but finally with excitement… and pride. I realised how far

I had come. There was no way anxiety was going to ruin this opportunity!!! Right at the top of my packing list was *My Wellness Toolbox*. It didn't let me down.

... And I have just returned from a fantastic long weekend in Ibiza for my sister's 40th birthday with a group of 12 lovely ladies, eight of whom I met for the first time on this holiday. This naturally made me a little apprehensive before we set off. Once again, the tools were packed in the ridiculous oversized bag for a weekend away... and although the tools (along with the four pairs of space-wasting shoes) didn't get much use, the overindulgence and late nights did make me call upon Tool #1 – Water most mornings! I took the chance to use Tool #2 – Breathe proactively in the adults-only hotel (amazing) and I am very grateful to have returned from Ibiza with some extra strength for Tool #14 – Positive People. Every single female on that trip had an inspirational story to share which in turn every single one of us embraced, supported and, when required, we laughed out loud... Tool #23 – Laughter working for us all.

These are a few more tools to help you overcome the stress and anxiety of going on holiday:

TOOL #2 BREATHE

When your mind travels towards 'negative' as you contemplate all things 'holiday' that you need to do and you start to become overwhelmed, try a few breathing exercises to help redirect your mind towards feelings of calm.

Sit comfortably with your feet on the ground, close

your eyes and try to visualise a destination that makes you feel positive. Then proceed to do the 'in for five, out for ten' breathing exercise. Keep doing it until you feel calm and the negative thoughts have subsided.

On your travels do this exercise at any time you start to feel anxious or overwhelmed... or even when you are sipping a cocktail at the side of the pool feeling relaxed. That is the perfect time to practise using this tool, so when you do have a moment of need it will kick in more easily.

TOOL #3 MUSIC

A holiday playlist with all your favourite mood-boosting songs will not only make the packing process easier but the songs will uplift you and make you feel more positive about the adventure ahead. You can then call upon the playlist at any time throughout your journey. To override any negative thinking turn the volume upwards and let the happy tunes take over.

TOOL #9 DAILY SELF-CARE

Preparing for a holiday is the perfect excuse to indulge in some extra daily self-care.

In the weeks leading up to a break in a warmer climate I always treat myself to one of my favourite body scrubs and add it to the morning shower routine to help my skin get holiday-ready. Just adding that extra one-minute step can make me feel like I am doing something positive towards my holiday.

If you struggle to find the time, book it in the diary and make it just as important as everything else you have got going on. Prioritise. Make time for *you*. Take complete advantage of this tool and get holiday-ready!

TOOL #15 GRATITUDE

In your diary add lots of gratitude and thank yous against the holiday dates.

Every morning leading up to the holiday, wake up and before you even get out of bed, be thankful for the holiday you have booked and that you *will* enjoy. Try and allow the excitement to build gradually. Call upon Tool #11 – Affirmations if you need to override any negative thoughts with sunshine ones.

If your holiday appears in a brochure, cut out the pictures and add them to your gratitude vision board.

… And at the end of your amazing experience do not forget to be thankful for the memories and the ones that will follow.

TOOL #22 PHYSICAL EXERCISE

Eating healthier and pulling out Tool #22 in the weeks running up to your break away will most likely uplift you, can make you feel more body-confident and normally results in improved sleep, which you will no doubt need to top up on if you are lucky enough to be heading to Ibiza!!

TOOL #26 ME (THAT'S YOU!)

This is an opportunity to have some downtime, a much-deserved break from the daily routine. Give yourself a break and value this time for *you*.

… And when you remember to pack the toothbrush…

**don't forget to pack Your Wellness Toolbox! …
And have a fabulous time!!**

Talking Tools Blog: Originally published June 2018

TOOL #30
THE BEACH

Oh, I do love to be beside the seaside.

I remember when I first read my paperback copy of *My Wellness Toolbox*, as soon as I closed the book and placed it on the table, with a little proud smile on my face, I flared my nostrils. I thought of a tool that was missing. The Beach. How could I have missed the beach that I have gone to so many times to help chill me out? The beach where I can often be found talking to pebbles. My haven.

Being near the sea is relaxing. The sound of the waves drenching the sand calms me down so easily. It is no surprise that research has proven that the sound of the waves alters our brain patterns, which encourages us to go into a deeper relaxed state, rejuvenating our body and mind.

When by the sea I find it easier to open my mind, therefore problem-solving and decision-making also come so much more easily.

Just being on the beach encourages me to pull out Tool #22 – Physical Exercise. If I have something weighing on my mind, a good walk along my favourite beach in Pembrokeshire, chatting to a pebble in hand, always helps. Regardless if the sun is shining and warming my skin, or if it's raining (and it is always that, you know, really wet stuff in Wales) or even if it feels like a tornado may blow me away, I'll take a walk, it always helps.

I have been known to run on the beach, although it does not happen often. I imagine the spectators using their laughter tool as I try to navigate running on sand probably get more benefit from it than me.

You may also enjoy a swim in the sea. I tend to avoid this at my haven; it is in South West Wales, my lips go blue at the thought of it. Freezing. Although you may find me dipping my toe in whilst releasing my pebbles (with any worries I have downloaded) into the waves.

However, when abroad I do like to take a proactive dip as I know the health benefits of warm seawater. It can activate the body's healing mechanisms to fight a number of different conditions and inflammatory diseases, as well as common aches and pains. This is also the reason why I often soak in Dead Sea, Epsom or Himalayan salt baths; the vitamins and minerals in saltwater bring a wealth of benefits for our immunity and are great for flushing away the negative toxins.

Oh the benefits of being on the beach are endless; I know one day we will leave the Midlands behind to be closer to the sea, but until then (I reckon I have at least another 15 years of trying to convince my husband to go sooner) I will embrace every opportunity I can to head to a beach and let this tool recharge me.

Get your flip-flops (or wellies) ready, it is beach time.

When I feel like I need this tool, but I can't get to it (for example, when the Government announces a lockdown), I will do a simple internet search to find 'the sounds of the sea' and fall asleep listening to one of my most favourite sounds in the world (note: this also proves useful for screaming babies).

Effectiveness: 10/10. The beach makes me feel good every time.

Ease: ?/10. This really does depend on how close you live to a beach or how often you get to go on a trip or holiday to one.

Cost: Depends. Again, this really does depend on how close you live to a beach or how often you get to go on a trip or holiday to one.

BEST
ESCAPE
ANYONE
CAN
HAVE

TOOL #31
SUNSETS

I am very grateful to have experienced so many incredible sunsets in my lifetime. I always feel so calm when I simply sit and just be 'in the moment' as the sun slowly falls, melting away the day. The beauty of a sunset always makes me smile.

Watching a sunset also encourages you to go outside, gives you time to connect with nature and allows you to take in some fresh air. All good for the soul.

I mostly use this tool alongside Tool #30 – The Beach, a powerful combination, but it is not essential. Simply absorbing the sunset on your commute home from work can also help you process and release some of the stresses of the day.

All good for your emotional wellbeing.

Effectiveness: 10/10. A sunset never fails to soothe me.

Ease: 7/10. The weather can be a slight blocker here in the UK, as can your location. Yet when you are in the right place, at the right time and the weather is fine, it is so easy to use this tool. Also, *do* be careful when watching sunsets, as it can be dangerous to stare *directly* at the sun, even as it is rising or setting.

Cost: Free

RAINY DAYS & MONDAYS

It is Monday. It is raining. Do rainy days and Mondays always get you down? (Carpenters song now playing in my head, most likely for the rest of the day!)

For some, Mondays and rain alone can trigger stress, worry, anxiety and the dread that today is going to be a bad day.

Since birth you may have been taught by a number of influencers that Mondays are tough, and rain is grey and miserable.

If you have been taught it (most likely unintentionally) by parents, family, teachers, caregivers... the media... you most likely believed it. Therefore, it has most likely become your reality. Your brain is wired to feel negative at just the thought of Mondays and rainy days. This will then trigger the thought patterns and behaviours that don't make you feel good and the negative cycle begins...

So, *what if* you can break that cycle?

What if we pull out Tool #20 and learn something new, rewire your thought process, change your thinking and retrain your brain?

What if we pull out Tool #9 and add some extra daily self-care to Monday morning routines to start the day on a more positive note?

What if we pull out Tool #15 and be thankful for the rain? Be grateful for what it helps and not what you feel it hinders?

What if on a Monday we choose to put on our sparkly boots and dance in the rain?

That is exactly what my two-year-old wanted to do this morning. She put her wellies on (the wrong way around) and stood at the back door asking to play in the rain.

I initially said, "No, Mummy's got to do her (Monday) jobs and we can't play in the rain," and as I walked back to the kitchen, I challenged my own answer. *Why?*

Why do I have to do my jobs now? (I don't.)

Why can't we play in the rain? (We can.)

What?

What will happen if the jobs are not done right now? (The jobs will not get done – the world won't stop.)

What will happen if we get wet in the rain? (We will get wet in the rain – we won't dissolve.)

I realised I am teaching my forever-absorbing two-year-old that we can't have fun on Monday mornings or play in the rain. Why?

I turned back around, put on my shoes, opened the back door and we went and jumped in muddy puddles.

It put the biggest smile on her little scrumptious face and Tool #23 – Laughter came flying out for us both… even when she decided to take her sparkly boots off as she wanted to run around on the wet grass in her socks… but, hey, why not?!

I challenge you on the next rainy day to go and jump in muddy puddles, dance in the rain, or do something silly that will make you smile and turn your Monday (or any day) the right way up.

Oh, that's right, it's Monday, so you haven't got the time. JFYI: it takes seconds to jump in a puddle! (Maybe a little longer to dry off.)

What if you could love your Mondays and rainy days?

Never underestimate that Tool #26 – ME (That's YOU!) can make the changes and choices to start loving them, or at least like them a little more than you do right now. Just watch what positive impact it has on *you*.

Talking Tools Blog: Originally published September 2019

YOUR MUSIC

Back in the 90s on a Sunday afternoon I would sit patiently listening to the Radio 1 Top 40, waiting to hit 'record' when my favourite songs played and pause when there was chat, creating my very own compilation tape. I realise now I've been making positive playlists all my life, I just did not realise it. They have always been a good thing for me.

What is on your positive playlist?

List the Top 10 songs that put a smile on your face, remind you of great times, give you a boost of energy and make you feel positive.

1.

2.

3.

4.

5.

6.

7.

8.

9.

10.

Do you have a peaceful playlist?

Think of five songs, instrumental music, or even meditations you would put on your peaceful playlist to help you relax, especially at bedtime (the same music may appear in your positive playlist).

1.

2.

3.

4.

5.

TOOL #32
GUIDED MEDITATION

Meditating has been scientifically proven to help you stress less, reduce anxiety, increase mental clarity and focus, help you relax and improve sleep and can be used to develop a positive mindset. Ultimately a power tool for both your physical and mental health.

However, meditations and my overthinking brain never used to get on. The overthinking brain won every time. I really struggled to switch off; any attempt to meditate would be railroaded by the overactive imagination and inability to think about 'nothing'. So, after a few failed attempts I gave up trying and that is why it was not a tool in My Wellness Toolbox.

Then in November 2018 I would discover my understanding of meditation was all wrong.

I thought that meditating would allow me to completely switch off the negative thinking, to block the intrusive thoughts, stop them in their tracks, when they went on their abusive attack. I thought meditation was a tool to escape from the negative thinking. *Wrong.*

Meditation is a power tool to retrain the brain to accept thoughts for exactly what they are. Just thoughts. To retrain the brain to just allow the thoughts to wander past without triggering a physical or emotional response.

Also, it is a skill that requires regular practice; giving up after a few attempts is why this tool had not previously worked for me.

Ironically, I had been 'overthinking' meditation and I was also holding on to the outdated belief, "Well, I tried this before, it doesn't work for me, so no point trying again."

Thanks to the encouragement of Claire Cross, an online fitness and wellbeing coach, I decided to give this tool another go. Claire had suggested guided meditations may help me when I was struggling to switch off at the end of busy and exciting days. She pointed me in the direction of the Headspace app (one of hundreds of meditation apps to choose from).

The Headspace app is simple to use. Tick. The first guided meditation I tried was only five minutes. Tick. The Headspace man's voice is lovely. Tick.

The first time I used it I fell asleep before it finished... and continued to fall asleep every time I listened to that lovely soothing voice of the Headspace man. It also helped me learn to meditate. Finally, this tool was working for me.

Listening to the guided meditations became part of the daily routine (I even manage to stay awake now... sometimes). I did some research and discovered another wonderful app called Breethe. This is jam-packed with guided meditations, bedtime stories for adults and relaxing tracks to choose from. A ready-made peaceful playlist.

You do not have to download an app or pay money for meditations, simply do an internet search on 'guided meditation' and you will find thousands online. Narrow the choice down by including a reason as to why you would like to meditate. For example, 'guided meditation to... let go... unwind... sleep... motivate... laugh... just be'.

When my mental health was declining at a rapid rate in 2019, I was calling upon guided meditations several times a day to help reduce the anxiety when I was leaving the house. They really did help.

More recently, during the Covid-19 lockdown and the anxieties that it brings, I have been using them most evenings to help me switch off and encourage a restful night's sleep. On the nights I have been disturbed (most likely by the three-year-old who fancies a chat) and struggled to resettle, I've switched on a meditation; it helps us all return to sleep (even the chatterbox).

Guided meditations are a powerful mindset tool. In November 2019 I was still struggling daily with negative and intrusive thoughts. Thinking this could help me, my lovely friend Liz invited me to do the Abundance Challenge, a 21-day guided meditation program by Deepak Chopra (Chopra Centre). The aim of the challenge is to help you develop a mindset of prosperity and abundance in your daily life by working with a series of short meditations for 21 days.

I nearly declined the invite. Could I be bothered? Did I have the energy?

I guessed that maybe it could help. I'm so glad I did, as not only did I love the soothing tones of Deepak's voice (another one that helps me sleep), this challenge really encouraged me to use Tool #15 – Gratitude every day. It also seemed to work, as abundance also did flow more easily in many areas of my life. By Christmas 2019 I was feeling significantly better compared to the previous months. I do believe this challenge played a healthy part in my improved mindset at that time.

I am so glad I gave this tool another chance. It really has helped me gain a healthier perspective on my own thoughts which has led to less self-sabotage and higher self-esteem.

There are different types of meditation; the guided meditations with visualisation work for me. Do some research, try different ones and work out what works for you.

Effectiveness: 8/10. Guided meditations can really help me unwind and relax, especially after a busy and stress-inducing day.

Ease: 6/10. Practice is required. Now that I have put the effort in to learn this skill, I find it very easy to simply switch on, breathe and let my worries pass me by.

Cost: Free – £7.00 per month (for some apps – based on my own research).

"Life gives you plenty of time to do whatever you want to do if you stay in the present moment."

(Deepak Chopra)

INTERVIEWS

Job interviews can make even the most laid-back and easy-going candidates nervous, that is why the tools in My Wellness Toolbox are not just for those that struggle with stress or anxiety. These tools can be used by anyone, to help you feel calmer and more focused when walking into the interview room.

Again, as I look down the list of tools I realise most of them will have been used in some way for interviews, so I have narrowed it down to the ten (OK, make that twelve) that have proved the most useful over the years.

TOOL #1 WATER

Make sure you are hydrated before heading into the interview. Take a bottle of water with you or ask for a glass of water on arrival. If the mouth starts to get dry with all that talking about how wonderful you are then take a few sips; it will help you keep calm.

TOOL #2 BREATHE

If you start to feel nervous before or during the interview remember to use your breathing exercises to help keep you calm. The one I use:

Breathe in for five. Breathe out for ten.

- Make sure your feet are on the ground
- Try and breathe in through your nose and out through your mouth
- Take a deep breath in and count to five
- Take a deep breath out and count to ten
- Repeat this until you feel calmer

Obviously, you may not be able to take the time out to do this during the interview, but if at any point you become overwhelmed or confused by a question, ask the interviewer to repeat the question and take those few seconds to take a deep breath and reset.

TOOL #3 MUSIC

When getting ready for the interview turn the music on and turn it up. Let your positive playlist uplift you and give you a boost of confidence.

TOOL #4 NO MEDIA

Unless beneficial for the interview try to keep the media switched off beforehand (this includes the Facebook feed!!!). Remain focused on all things positive. Sometimes reading or watching something negative on the news could upset, worry or distract you and result in unwanted concerns when trying to remain focused.

TOOL #5 ESSENTIAL OILS

A blend of rosemary and lavender is perfect for interviews; not only will this powerful combination put you in a good mood, but it can also reduce stress levels and can even help your emotions deal with the situation better. Either inhale the oils using a diffuser, rub some in your skin using a carrier oil (I use coconut oil) or if your skin allows, dab some on your wrists or behind your ears… this may also benefit (or even sway) the interviewers! Wink.

TOOL #8 RESCUE REMEDY

If the butterflies are dancing around before the interview, then a quick drop or spray of Rescue Remedy before you enter the interview can help settle the nerves.

TOOL #9 DAILY SELF-CARE

Book some time in your diary for the days leading up to the interview to have some 'me' time and make sure you stick to it. The evening before an interview I book myself in for a bath with lavender essential oils; it helps me unwind and helps me sleep. I will also try to have an early night.

I also do that thing my mum used to do when we were kids and lay out my interview outfit on a bed the night before and make sure I have got everything in my bag; this makes the interview day start with fewer things to think about.

TOOL #11 AFFIRMATIONS

Write them down, stick them up somewhere visible and repeat. Repeat. Repeat.

- I am attracting the right opportunities to my life.
- I am the perfect candidate for this job.
- I find job interviews easy.

TOOL #13 SELF-HELP BOOKS

If the nerves are really kicking in, I automatically reach for the Calm Anchor tool that I learned from Paul McKenna's self-help book *Control Stress: Stop Worrying and Feel Good Now!*

The Calm Anchor is an associative conditioning tool. In simple terms, the Calm Anchor exercises from the book enabled me to train my brain to respond in a certain way when I performed a specific action. Now when in nervous situations if I press my thumb and middle finger together my head is flooded with positive thoughts about myself and can make me instantly calmer and more positive.

TOOL #15 GRATITUDE

In your diary write "Thank you for everything working out for me" against the interview date.

At every stage of the process show gratitude to everyone you deal with.

If you have a Tool #7 – Gratitude Vision Board, why not stick up a picture of the company logo you want to work with, and every day leading up to the interview be grateful for the opportunities that lie ahead with that company.

… And don't forget to thank yourself for getting to the interview stage in the first place.

TOOL #25 WRITING

Preparing answers for the more predictable interview questions always gives me a confidence boost. Grab a notepad and a pen and scribble some notes; this can also help you release any pre-interview nerves.

"Why are you the right person for this job?" "What are your strengths?" "What are the key skills you can bring to this role?" This encourages you to write down all things positive about yourself.

"What would you say is one of your weaknesses?" I try and respond with a 'weakness' that also highlights a 'strength', for example "I sometimes find it hard to delegate as I like to take ownership of a task right to the end. I am aware of the impact this can have on my own wellbeing and am consciously making efforts to delegate more."

TOOL #26 ME (THAT'S YOU!)

You got the interview. *You* are skilled. *You* are talented. *You* are good at what you do. *You* can do this. *You* have got this!!

Good luck!

Talking Tools Blog: Originally published October 2018

YOUR AFFIRMATIONS

Affirmations are positive quotes/statements/phrases that you can repeat to yourself out loud or in your head, reminding yourself or telling yourself how you want to feel, what you want to be and even what you want to achieve. You can also write your favourite ones down, put them in your purse, hang them on your wall, stick them on your desk at work and include them on your vision boards; just make them very present in your life.

I have used affirmations throughout my life to override negative thinking with positive thoughts. Anxiety can riddle your mind with negative thinking that can be scary and eventually rip apart your self-confidence; it can be a vicious circle. I learned to interrupt those negative thoughts with positive affirmations; it really does work. Positivity does not have to be the exception; it can be the rule. Affirmations can really support the rebuilding of your confidence.

Use the space below to create
your very own affirmation.

A few simple steps to take to create one:

1. Write down a reoccurring negative thought you have that upsets you, triggers anxiety and/or is holding you back (e.g. I can't do it, I'm not attractive, I'm useless, I can't afford it)
2. Write down the opposite of that negative thought
3. Cross out the negative thought
4. You now have a positive affirmation
5. **Repeat. Repeat. Repeat.**

MY WELLNESS TOOLBOX – 1
ANXIETY – 0

Talking Tools Blog
11 October 2019

Yesterday I woke up, after three hours' broken sleep due to my poorly two-year-old, feeling anxious. On what should be an exciting day the adrenaline was pumping but not in the way I needed it to be... and then the negative chatter started (and revisited several times)... followed by heart palpitations... a bit more adrenaline surged in... nausea showed its sickening face... frustration popped in... irritability... burping... appetite decided to disappear... overwhelming feelings tried to stop me starting the car. Fortunately, I had My Wellness Toolbox.

Although I had to work very hard with multiple tools yesterday (using them reactively), they ultimately got me to Solihull Radio station to deliver my very first and very important #TeamTalk show for World Mental Health Day... and got me through the show. When I got home, I admit I didn't celebrate, I cried with relief (and frustration).

I feel it is important that I am honest with you. For some, you may watch My Wellness Toolbox journey and think I always use my tools proactively, that I've got it all sorted and under control; I have not. Yesterday my current mental health, fear and anxiety nearly beat me. *But it didn't* (I believe it would have 13 years ago).

Yesterday was a tough day and by the end of it I was exhausted from overriding the negative, frustrated that anxiety is knocking down my door once more after 13 years, yet I am extremely grateful that I had my tools so I didn't miss out on such an amazing opportunity. I must have done something right; it was confirmed that I am the new Wellness Presenter for Solihull Radio and will be hosting a weekly show.

These are the tools that I pulled out yesterday. As you can see My Wellness Toolbox was extremely busy.

Tool #1 Water
Tool #2 Breathe
Tool #3 Music – Turn It Up
Tool #4 Media – Turn It Off
Tool #5 Essential Oils
Tool #8 Rescue Remedy

Tool #9 Daily Self-Care

Tool #11 Affirmations

Tool #13 Self-Help Books

Tool#14 Positive People

Tool #15 Gratitude

Tool #16 Let Go & Release Techniques

Tool #17 Reiki

Tool #18 The Secret

Tool #20 Learn Something New

Tool #26 ME (That's YOU!)

Can any of these tools help you?

TOOL #33
YES

I know, I know… in *My Wellness Toolbox* I talked about the importance of pulling out Tool #12 – NO to give me breathing space and to help set boundaries. That has not changed. However, what dawned on me more recently was that saying 'yes' over the years has been just as important for my mental health, self-confidence and mindset.

In August 2018 a very excited and nervous me was sat in the Solihull Radio studio being interviewed by the radio station owner, Geoff O'Brien. It was the release date of *My Wellness Toolbox*. Just a few weeks later I was sat in the same studio recording the audiobook version; the lovely Geoff had very kindly offered to do this for me at no cost. I absolutely loved both experiences. I joked to my husband that one day I would love to be a radio presenter. We both laughed. Ridiculous idea… right?

As I had been a guest on a show, a year later in August 2019, I was invited to a Solihull Radio relaunch party to celebrate their location move. I was unable to attend but I did respond to the invitation to ask if they had any plans to promote awareness of World Mental Health Day. Geoff suggested I pop into the studio and help brainstorm some ideas. I left that brainstorming session on a September afternoon as the new Wellness Presenter for Solihull Radio. The first show would be co-presenting with Geoff for a special World Mental Health Day show. Boom. Not quite sure how that happened.

I was overwhelmed, proud, honoured, smiling, may have done a little jump in the air as I left the studio… and most importantly excited that I was going to be able to share the tools in My Wellness Toolbox via the power of radio to help others.

Yet there was a huge 'What if?' cloud hanging over my head. My mental health had been declining. What if this makes me worse? What if I'm terrible? What if I am a fraud? What if I can't do it? What if they have got it wrong? What if I fail? What if people laugh at me? What if I'm no good? What if I am useless? What if this is a trap? … Cue intrusive, irrational thoughts. What if I should have said 'no'?

Ironically, I had extremely bad anxiety for that very first show on World Mental Health Day, the worst I had experienced for years. On the way to the studio I was working so hard to override the negative chatterbox telling me to turn back home, telling me I was a fraud. Water, affirmations, Rescue Remedy, breathing exercises, the positive playlist and so many more got me into the studio.

We had a panel of guests talking tools for mental health. I found it very difficult to concentrate; I physically shook all the way through the show. I felt like an imposter. A fraud. How can I be doing a show on mental health when mine is declining at a rapid rate? When I got home that evening I fell onto the sofa and balled my eyes out. I really wanted to do this but what if it wasn't the right time? What if I should have said 'no'?

A few weeks later in November, *The Wellness Wednesday Show* was launched. Each week I would be sharing stories, talking tools and adding songs to the positive playlist with guests who either worked in the wellness industry or had their very own mental health and wellness journey to share to help others. I very nearly pulled out, yet something in my gut was telling me to persevere. Something was telling me to keep saying 'yes'.

I am so glad I did. Over the coming weeks *The Wellness Wednesday Show* would not only be received very well by the radio listeners, it would become part of my therapy towards feeling more positive again.

Geoff empowered and trusted me to plan, produce and present all the shows. This enabled me to pull out Tool #20 – Learn Something New, which gave me something positive to focus on and helped start to rebuild my self-esteem and confidence.

They say everyone comes into your life for a reason; if I ever doubted this, I certainly do not now. Not only have

I made some great friends on the Solihull Radio team, to date there have been 40 *Wellness Wednesday Shows* recorded. Every single one of the guests that has shared their stories on the show, the majority of whom I had never met before, has helped me with my mental health in some way, without them realising. That is the power of Tool #27 – Talking.

They handed me new power tools, made me step back into my past to face my fears, updated my positive playlist, encouraged me to change my mindset, put a smile on my face, and some have even become friends. Tool #14 – Positive People is more charged than ever.

Saying 'yes' to the opportunity was the right thing to do. I doubted myself; on some days I still do. Yet I look at the evidence. I look at what has been achieved. I look at the positive people I am surrounded by. I look at my overflowing toolbox. So, until further notice I will keep saying 'yes'.

If you really want to do something but you are not sure if you can do it, try saying 'yes'. It may just lead you to exactly where you want to be.

Effectiveness: 8/10. Saying 'yes' to the things you really want to do can boost your confidence and lead you to many more positive opportunities.

Ease: 6/10. It is not always easy to say 'yes', especially if fear, other people and other potential obstacles are blocking your way. Yet if you can pull out some of your other tools to help move those blockers out the way and can say 'yes' to the things that are right for you, life may just become what you want it to be.

Cost: Free – £, depends on what you are saying 'yes' to.

Thank you to all the guests who have joined me on *The Wellness Wednesday Show*. Thank you for sharing your stories, talking tools, adding some amazing music to the positive playlist and for being positive people in My Wellness Toolbox.

All shows are available as podcasts and can be downloaded on PodBean, Spotify, Apple Podcasts, Google and other podcast networks.

Guest	Company / Role	Content	Date broadcast
Liz Stanford	**The Calm Birth School** Owner, Mindset Coach & Confidence Creator	Living with postnatal depression and the challenges of parenthood	20 November 2019
Victoria Obermaier	**Victoria Obermaier Coaching** Mindset Coach	The importance of self-love, rebuilding self-confidence and practising gratitude	27 November 2019
Claire Cross	**Claire Cross Fitness & Wellbeing** Coach	Fitness and wellbeing tools to empower you	4 December 2019
Glenn Mantle	Corporate IT Manager	Living with health anxiety	11 December 2019
Holly Matthews	**The Happy Me Project** Life & Mindset Coach	Finding happiness through grief	8 January 2019
Caroline Gibbs	**Coaching Together** Life Coach	Living with alcohol addiction and the road to recovery	15 January 2020

Frank Sinclair	**Fit with Frank** Personal Trainer	Fitness for all the family	22 January 2020
Martin Pemberton	**Just 1 to 11 It** Personal Trainer, Coach & Mental Health Advocate	Just 1 to 11 It: wellness recovery plan to overcome anxiety and depression	29 January 2020
Lizzy Bernthal	**Release Your Potential** Life Coach	Empowerment, resilience and psychological wellbeing	4 February 2020
Hannah Martinig	**Hannah Martinig Photography** Photographer	The importance of body confidence to improve mental health	12 February 2020
Jackie Breen	**Solihull Reiki** Holistic Therapist	Reiki therapy to overcome stress-related illness	19 February 2020

Kerry Hearsey	**Life Architect Coaching** Mental Health Author & Life Coach	Dealing with a mental health misdiagnosis and mental health books for children	26 February 2020
Leila Holmes	**Physioadvantage** Physiotherapist	Physiotherapy for women's antenatal and postnatal health	4 March 2020
Estelle Keeber	**Immortal Monkey** Founder, Entrepreneur & Author	Turning your life around after experiencing domestic violence and living with depression	11 March 2020
Katie Isles & Ava Thomson	**Two Blonde Brummies** Professional Models & YouTube Channel Presenters	Two become three to talk tools for mental health and wellness	25 March 2020
Aoife Madden	**'B is for Bladder'** Teacher & Blogger	Living with a chronic illness and invisible disability	29 April 2020

Hannah Poulton	**HLP Therapy** Physiotherapist, Acupuncturist & Scar Therapist	Benefits of scar therapy, acupuncture and physiotherapy on both mental and physical health	6 May 2020
Laura Bland	**Laura B Fitness** Coach, Mentor & Author	Fitness, body confidence and self-love	13 May 2020
Kate Moxley	**Kate Moxley Wellness For All** Mental Health First Aid England Instructor & Mental Health Advocate	Mental health awareness special. Talking tools for Covid-19 anxieties	20 May 2020
Lee Jones & Jim Roper	**Silhillians RUFC** Chairman & Commercial Lead	Life following a catastrophic and life-changing spinal injury	27 May 2020
Tammy Rolfe	**Motivated Mummies** Life Coach	Overcoming crippling anxiety and social phobia	3 June 2020

Katie Washbourne & Michelle O'Connor	**Ordinary Magic** Founder & Director	Children's mental health	10 June 2020
Emma Hunter	**Carers Trust** Volunteer Co-Ordinator	Focus on the Carers Trust and life as a carer	17 June 2020
Tania Taylor	**Tania-Taylor. co.uk** Clinical Hypnotherapist and Psychotherapist	A Guided Meditation with Tania Taylor	17th June 2020
Gregory Weston	**NHS** Volunteer & Mental Health Advocate	Life following a serious and life-changing brain injury	24 June 2020
Mel Wakeman	**Wakeman Nutrition** Nutritionist, Coach & Mentor	Nutrition and relationships with food	1 July 2020
Tristan Lee	**Tristanlee.com** Gorgeousness Coach	Recovery from a nervous breakdown to empowering others to age gorgeously inside and out	8 July 2020

Fay Smith	**House of Hair Hostess** Salon Owner & Solihull Radio Presenter	Life story. Overcoming rejection by biological father	15 July 2020
Asha Adutwim	**Asha Amour** Self-Love and Divine Power Transformational Therapist	A panel of women in business sharing their self-love tools	22 July 2020
Anya Pendlebury	**Sofya Style Magazine** Owner & Editor		
Mel Wakeman	**Wakeman Nutrition** Anti-Diet Nutritionist		
Sarah Meharg	**Moodlifter Award winning** Occupational Therapist and Personal Trainer	Improving mental and physical health through physical exercise	29 July 2020

Angie Freel (COGS)	**Cogs Self-Development Book Club** Founder and self-development advocate	Building self-development into your life quickly and easily	5 August 2020
Avnita Suri	**Freedom from Chronic Pain** Lifestyle Prescriptions Health Coach	Overcome chronic pain using mind body healing techniques	12 August 2020
Jennifer Emery	**The Dance Club at Home** Founder and Fitness Coach	How dance and exercise can help you heal from life traumas	19 August 2020
Sara Fenandes	**Only Human Therapy** Holistic Therapist, Emotional Healer and Motherhood Mentor	Maternal Mental Health and recovery from postpartum psychosis	26 August 2020

Natalie Scarlett	**The Black Heritage Support Service** Founder	Focus on the BHHS and why it was set up to support the Black community during the Covid-19 Pandemic	2 September 2020
Laura Moss	**Inspire & Connect Networking** Entrepreneur and Founder of Inspire & Connect	How the Covid-19 pandemic and a need to adapt businesses, led to a journey of self-discovery	9 September 2020
Suneta Bagri	**Cultivate Coaching & Consultancy Every Teacher Matters Project** Founder & Director	Supporting Teachers and their mental health	16 September 2020

Richard Kirby	**Rich Kirby Elite Performance** Strength, Conditioning & Rehabilitation Coach	The importance of the mind and body connection to overcome physical and mental illness	23 September 2020
Josie Williamson	**Pursue Your Purpose Coaching** Personal Performance Coach		
Gulshen Bano	**Strike Back Self Defence for Women** Founder & Instructor	How a terminal cancer diagnosis led to learning new skills, alternative therapies, a healthier lifestyle and a new career.	30 September 2020

I have a sudden urge to keep using Tool #15 – Gratitude…

Thank you to Geoff O'Brien (Solihull Radio Station Director) for the amazing opportunity for me to produce and present *The Wellness Wednesday Show* and for giving me the freedom to be creative.

Thank you to Richard Davies (Solihull Radio Creative Director), for being *The Wellness Wednesday Show* No. 1 fan, encouraging me on those anxious days at the beginning of my Solihull Radio journey and for all your creative input to promote the show and *My Wellness Toolbox*.

Thank you to Jas Rohel (Solihull Radio Presenter), for your friendship and support, Wednesdays would not be the same without you in the studio.

Thank you to Mathew Spencer (Solihull Radio Technical Director), for answering my stupid questions and for your patience!!

Thank you to Aline Boblin (former Solihull Radio Station Development) for your ongoing support of *The Wellness Wednesday Show* and all things *My Wellness Toolbox*.

Thank you to every single member of the Solihull Radio team. I am very grateful to be part of such a great and expanding team of incredible presenters.

There are so many great, informative, positive and fun shows broadcast on Solihull Radio. Take a look at the website www.solihullradio.com for the full schedule and to listen in live; you may just find a new tool for Your Wellness Toolbox.

"If someone offers you an amazing opportunity and you're not sure you can do it, say yes – then learn how to do it!"

(Richard Branson)

PUBLIC EVENTS

For my birthday this year my husband surprised me with a night away to London to watch *Mamma Mia!* at the theatre. For many this is a wonderful and exciting thing to do, I now agree, yet less than 12 years ago the thought of going to the theatre, a concert, the cinema, a big sporting event or any kind of public event would fill me with dread, nausea and anxiety.

In 2007 shortly after we started dating, he surprised me with a weekend to London to watch Take That at the O2 Arena. He went to so much effort, even arranging with my manager for me to have the afternoon off work so he could execute his exciting plan. However, even I wasn't prepared for my reaction. The poor bloke thought he was doing something romantic and amazing for me, but instead of jumping on him when the surprise was revealed, it left me terrified and extremely anxious. Not only was I going to be facing a concert with large crowds, the trip involved a ride on the claustrophobic, no escape route London Underground!!! Panic! What was he thinking?!?!

It was that same bloke that took this reaction in his stride, and with his positive encouragement I made the decision to face the anxiety head on. That weekend the tools in My Wellness Toolbox, that I had picked up during the previous year, were used in full force and I also discovered some new tools that I still proactively use today.

Just recently our good friend was tasked with booking tickets for Kylie in concert later this year. We were thrilled when his text confirmed ticket success, but his text also alerted me to the fact the tickets are not seated. Standing at concerts is one fear I have yet to face in person and have consciously avoided several times. I immediately whipped out Tool #12 – NO and responded to advise that it was no problem, I would sell my ticket and miss out this time. Then after beating myself up for ten minutes I grabbed Tool #26 – ME (that's YOU!), gave myself a talking to and reminded myself that My Wellness Toolbox will always be by my side. I can do this.

If you get those extreme feelings of dread when attending similar public events, then these are some of the obvious tools in My Wellness Toolbox that could come in useful for you:

TOOL #1 WATER

My trusted bottle of water will always be in my hand on a trip to the theatre, cinema or concert. I may not drink from it, but I know that if I do start to feel dry-mouthed, nervous or anxious it is readily available to me.

TOOL #2 BREATHE

On the day if you start to worry or overthink negatively about the public event then pull out your Breathe Tool to help relax you and clear the mind.

At the event if you start to feel anxious you can use the breathing exercises to instantly calm you.

Breathe in for five. Breathe out for ten.

- Make sure your feet are on the ground
- Try and breathe in through your nose and out through your mouth
- Take a deep breath in and count to five
- Take a deep breath out and count to ten

It does not matter how quickly you count or for how long you do this exercise, just repeat this until you feel calmer.

TOOL #8 RESCUE REMEDY

Before the event a proactive drop or spray of Rescue Remedy will help you to remain calm. Pop it in your pocket and if your feelings do start to take over during the event another drop, or spray, will help resettle you. Available from most high street chemists and supermarkets.

TOOL #11 AFFIRMATIONS

Affirmations work very hard for me in this scenario especially if I have any doubts, worries or fears about the public event I am attending running through my head. I take the negative thoughts and I consciously replace them with a positive affirmation. Then repeat. Repeat. Repeat.

- Facing my fears means I am rising above them.
- I will embrace this event and the good memories it will bring me.
- My life is wonderful and brings me amazing opportunities.
- I can do this.

TOOL #14 POSITIVE PEOPLE

When attending any kind of public event that may put you on edge try and attend with the positive people in your life. Not the people that will ridicule, roll their eyes or ignore you if you do have a panic. They are not the positive people in your life. If they invite you to such an event, then try and pull out your NO tool.

Choose to attend with the ones that will support and uplift you. When we went to the Take That concert in 2007, that bloke that is now my husband didn't allow me to indulge in the anxiety I was experiencing, yet he didn't ignore it either, he simply told me to take each step as it came along and at any point we could leave. I was sick before the concert started but just knowing I had his backing if I wanted to escape was enough. So, I continued to the next step. Five minutes into the concert the fears and doubts (and thankfully the sickness) had been forgotten. Not only did I add him to My Wellness Toolbox that weekend but Take That's 'Rule the World' would also become a guarantee for the future positive playlist, and our first dance song!

… And just knowing I am going to the Kylie concert with positive people, ones that I know won't bat an eyelid if I have a wobble and need to step outside to take a few breaths, has already put me at ease about going.

TOOL #16 LET GO & RELEASE TECHNIQUES

Why do public events make you nervous, fearful or anxious? Can you let 'it' go?

Using the WIDABI technique (Write It Down And Burn It) may help you let go of the 'it' that is driving your worries and anxieties related to public events.

- On a piece of paper write down what you want to let go of. This may be a fear, a worry, a situation, a memory… a person… anything. We refer to it as 'it'.
- You can write down one word or a novel – up to you
- Be grateful for any lessons that you have learned from 'it'
- Say goodbye to any negativity 'it' created
- Release 'it' into the fire/flame/BBQ (just make sure it is safe to do so)

- Let 'it' go
- Watch 'it' physically burn away
- Feel the benefits within minutes/hours/days

I recognise that my fear of standing at concerts is related to an old and outdated belief that I need to be in control, and being part of a standing crowd means I have no control. I have absolutely no evidence or personal experience to support this. Time to WIDABI!!!

Combining this tool with the positive people in my life and knowing that I have all the above tools in My Wellness Toolbox, if needed, means I am confident I will be attending Kylie and any other public events anxiety-free this year. These tools may just do the same for you.

Have a great time!

Talking Tools Blog: Originally published October 2018

"You're not supposed to feel good all of the time and if you can find out why you hold the belief that you should, then you'll get good at feeling all of the time, which is much better. Read that again."

(Josh Connolly)

YOUR LIMITING & OUTDATED BELIEFS

Limiting and outdated beliefs are a collection of opinions and fearful thoughts about ourselves and others that hold us back in some way, prevent us from grabbing opportunities and can trigger worry, anxiety and other uncomfortable emotions. Turns out I have/had quite a few over the years.

These limiting beliefs have been formed at some point in our life by our unconscious mind. They will be based on life experiences, childhood trauma and, most often, past events that we may have misinterpreted in some way. The more we think these thoughts, the more they become cemented in our minds, the more we believe them, the more evidence we seem to dig up to support them, yet they are mostly untrue and do not serve us any positive purpose.

If we can let them go, this can significantly reduce the worry, the anxiety and in turn help build our confidence, boost our self-esteem and allow us to move forward and take action to do the things that these limiting beliefs have been holding us back from.

However, the tricky bit is that we don't always realise we have the limiting beliefs, yet when we work on digging them out, we can actually challenge them and reprogram our brain quite easily to let them go.

You may want to grab a notepad and pen to do this exercise.

The aim is to acknowledge a limiting belief that may be holding you back or creating the uncomfortable feelings and emotions for you, then take the steps to let it go, replacing it with the truth and empowering belief.

You can do this for any area of your life, career, relationships, finances, health:

Step 1: Discover, acknowledge and question the belief

What is currently holding you back?

Examples:

- I lack confidence.
- I am not good enough.
- I can't afford it.
- I don't have the support I need.
- I don't deserve it.

- I can't trust anyone.
- I'm too impatient / lazy / anxious / negative / annoying / <insert any other negative adjective>.

Is this really true?

Do you have concrete evidence this belief is true, or is it based on a past experience or what someone else has told you?

Do you acknowledge that this could be or is a limiting belief?

(When the answer is 'yes' move to Step 2!)

Step 2: Identify the source of this belief
Where did this belief come from?

Examples of the source:

- Childhood experiences.
- Relationships with family, friends or significant others.
- What you were taught by parents, teachers or caregivers.
- Experiences in the workplace.
- Random interactions.
- Something you overheard.
- Other people's thoughts and opinions.

A few examples of limiting beliefs and where they may have come from:

- I can't trust anyone in any relationship, people always betray me. My last partner cheated on me.
- I can't take the risk, my mum always used to say risk-takers are idiots. Play it safe. Every time.
- I am not going to follow my dreams because I am not good enough; my friends have always laughed at my ideas and told me to 'come back down to earth'.
- I can't lose weight easily, no one in my family can; my grandmother told me I will always have thunder thighs.
- Everyone is luckier than me; my friends earn more money than me and have bigger houses.

- I'm not brave enough to take my small children on holiday abroad; a lady I met on the train told me it is a real hassle and her children do not travel well on flights.

Step 3: Consider the reasons why the belief is false

Try to think of some of the reasons why the belief is false. For example:

- The belief came from someone else's experiences, concerns or fears. Not yours.
- The belief came from another's judgement or opinion.
- Not everybody is the same.
- You have never actually tried and therefore have no evidence it is true.
- It has never happened to you before.
- You have no evidence that it is true.
- You know deep down it is not true.

Step 4: Let go of the limiting belief

Write down: "I no longer believe <insert the limiting belief> is true. I am letting go of this limiting belief today."

Say it out loud. Repeat three times.

Step 5: Replace the limiting belief

Now it is time to replace the limiting belief with a positive message. This will be the opposite of the limiting belief.

A few examples:

- I am confident and *can do this.*
- I am good enough and *can do this.*
- I can afford it and it will come to me easily.
- I can find the support I need.
- I deserve it and always have done.
- I can trust others and have loving relationships.
- I am patient/motivated/carefree/positive/wonderful <insert lots of positive adjectives to describe you>.

Step 6: Repeat. Repeat. Repeat.

Continue to practise your new positive and empowering belief and check in with yourself that it is working. If it is not, then go back to the start and work on it some more (or see the note below).

Step 7: Go back to Step 1

… and do this for all those limiting beliefs that have been holding you back. You got this!

Talking therapy was the ideal place for me to work through the many outdated and limiting beliefs I had back in 2006 and again more recently. I worked through several exercises like this in those sessions. If you need help to dig out those limiting beliefs, I would recommend you explore the options for working with a qualified psychotherapist or coach to help you.

"You can't go back and question your past. You can only make your future."

(Matt Swift)

WEDDINGS & CELEBRATIONS

Watching the Royal Wedding I could not begin to imagine how nervous the bride (Meghan) and groom (Harry) must feel knowing the whole world was watching their momentous and beautiful occasion, with the media scrutinising every detail and commenting on every move they make.

It quickly led me to reflect on how anxious I used to feel about attending weddings. They are happy and exciting occasions for most, yet my excitement would often turn to panic as the big day approached. My biggest fear was that I would have a panic attack during the service and cause a scene; if I was part of the actual wedding party these feelings would intensify.

In the past ten years my tools have been used proactively for all the weddings I have attended, to keep the anxiety and nerves under control, as a guest, as a speaker, as a bridesmaid, and especially when I was the bride.

TOOL #1 WATER

This tool is always with me for the big stuff! As a guest I will slip a bottle in with me to the service. However, if delivering a reading or speech, or if you are part of the bridal party and therefore can't walk down the aisle with a bottle, chewing gum is a perfect alternative to prevent the dry mouth. Just try and avoid chewing it aggressively when the cameras are rolling; I learned this was not a good look as the bridesmaid at my best friend's wedding. Whoops!

The best men on our wedding day were given the task to ensure a bottle of water was available at the front of the church in case I needed to take a sip at any point. It didn't even cross my mind to take a sip when the service got underway but knowing it would be there put my nerves at ease before I walked down the aisle.

We also provided bottles of water for our guests as they left the church; we wanted to pass on the tool to anyone who may experience similar feelings. It turned out to be a very hot day, so this was very welcome by all.

TOOL #2 BREATHE

Tools 1 and 2 will show up for most scenarios... so as before, breathe in for five and breathe out for ten.

TOOL #4 NO MEDIA

If you are feeling overwhelmed, nervous or negative about attending a wedding the last thing you need is to read or watch anything negative as that will only intensify the feelings.

Keep the media switched off (as much as you can) and turn the positive playlist up whilst you are getting ready.

TOOL #5 ESSENTIAL OILS

To help aid a restful sleep the night before add a few drops of lavender to a pre-bed bath or on your pillow.

In the morning add a citrus-based blend to the diffuser, like lemon, sweet orange or grapefruit; these are all energising and will refresh and lift you ready for the day ahead.

TOOL #7 GRATITUDE VISION BOARD

Stick the wedding invitation up on your gratitude vision board and every time you spot it say 'thank you' for the good times ahead and the wonderful time you will have on the big day.

TOOL #8 RESCUE REMEDY

Pop it in the handbag or jacket pocket and if you start to feel stressed or panicky have a quick spray and it will help calm you down. Alternatively add a few drops to your bottle of water.

TOOL #16 LET GO & RELEASE TECHNIQUES

Using the Fear Release Technique could help you neutralise any worries or concerns you have ahead of the big day.

If you are the one getting married you can do this exercise with your spouse-to-be; you may even discover they are having similar feelings or worries or have the answer to put you at ease.

Without discussing, both write down anything that is making you feel anxious or worried about the big day. Then in turn have a chat about what you have written down, get it out there in the open and support each other through the discussion. Then for everything you have written down replace the concern, fear or worry with a positive affirmation – making great use of Tool #11 – Affirmations.

For example, on the run-up to our big day I did have a worry that past anxieties could rear their head on the big day and cause me to have a panic attack at the altar. This or a similar fear can be replaced with the affirmation "I will be calm and relaxed on my big day and will enjoy every moment." Repeat. Repeat. Repeat. Every day!

This technique can really help you open up and release all the unwanted thoughts and negative thinking, putting your mind at ease and reducing the chance of anxiety taking over on the day.

TOOL #23 LAUGHTER

Laughter and smiling are great medicines for mind and body; even when fake, they can immediately reduce stress levels. Weddings are the perfect time to wear your beautiful smile. Keep smiling, pass it on and it will help you and potentially maybe others feel less anxious... it may also attract Tool #14 – Positive People for you to enjoy the day with!

TOOL #26 ME (THAT'S YOU!)

When you are all dressed up and ready to go, smile at yourself, repeat any positive affirmations and thank yourself for all the new happy memories you will be making that day.

Go, enjoy yourself and have the most wonderful time.

Talking Tools Blog: Originally published June 2018

'HANGXIETY'

Hangovers happen, especially when you have that "Oh go on then, one more for the road" moment. It's great at the time but the next day the hangover arrives bringing a large helping of 'hangxiety'!

These are some of the tools that may help ease the negative feelings that hangxiety likes to throw up:

TOOL #1 WATER

Keep yourself hydrated. Good for you physically and helps clear the mind.

TOOL #2 BREATHE

Pull out your breathing exercises if the hangover is making you feel panicky.

TOOL #4 NO MEDIA

If you are feeling negative and your mind is racing don't encourage it to absorb any more negativity that is outside of your control that may make it feel worse.

TOOL #5 ESSENTIAL OILS

Citrus oils, like lemon and orange, are the perfect pick-me-up. Switch the diffuser on or drop some in the shower tray and let them uplift you.

TOOL #9 DAILY SELF-CARE

Do something simple that you know will make you feel better and recharge you. A bath? Positive playlist? Fruit smoothie? Walk in the fresh air? Full English breakfast...

... and the power tool that will help make a difference:

TOOL #10 ACCEPTANCE

The hangover is here, and it will pass. Don't beat yourself up for the overindulgence; accept what has gone before and know that you have got Your Wellness Toolbox with some great tools you can pull out to help you feel better.

Hangovers happen and many of us can overindulge on occasion, however if you are concerned that you or a loved one could be drinking too much alcohol and it is impacting your or their health and wellbeing you can seek more guidance and advice on https://www.drinkaware.co.uk/

Talking Tools Blog: Originally published September 2019

YOUR WELLNESS
CHALLENGES

Pick three of these challenges to complete in the next seven days:

Set a reminder on your phone or put them in your diary at the time you plan to do them.

- Drink two litres of water every day this week
- Practise a breathing exercise
- Create your very own positive playlist
- Digital detox for at least two hours today
- Enjoy a relaxing bath or shower with a few drops of lavender essential oils
- Phone a good friend for a chat
- Create a gratitude vision board

- Try a natural alternative for a wellness or health product in your home
- Book in some 'me' time and enjoy every moment
- Start to embrace the things that make you unique
- Create a new and personalised affirmation – make it visible in your home
- Say 'no' when you want to say 'no'
- Read a self-help book that will help you grow
- Make plans with a positive person in your life
- Write a list of ten things you are grateful for
- Let go and release with WIDABI (Write It Down And Burn It)
- Research complementary or alternative relaxation therapies and book an appointment (e.g. Reiki, reflexology)
- Write down three goals you want to achieve and believe you will achieve them. You will.
- Book an appointment for a massage or relaxing treatment
- Research something that interests you that you would like to know more about
- Carry out a random act of kindness
- Get active and move
- Watch your favourite comedy film or comedian
- Look in the mirror. Appreciate and love the person looking straight back at you.
- Write a love letter to yourself or a loved one

TOOL #34

CRYSTALS

At the start of 2020, following an anxious end to 2019, I decided to pull out Tool #20 – Learn Something New. This has always helped me regain some focus.

The more wellness events I attend, the more it becomes apparent how many of you have already got crystals in Your Wellness Toolbox.

I had always been intrigued by crystals and crystal healing yet had never really 'got it' and used to feel quite overwhelmed at the thought of trying to 'get it'. It is a never-ending subject, so much to learn.

In May 2019 whilst on holiday in 'our happy place' our five-year-old asked me if I could take him to a shop so he could buy a crystal as he liked the one I had next to my bedside. I took him to a lovely Pembrokeshire gift shop where they had a huge array of beautiful crystals; he was fascinated by all of them (and so was I). He chose a clear calcite.

When he was heading to bed that evening, he asked if he could sleep with his new crystal as "I think it will keep the nightmares away".

"*What?!?!*" We did not know he was having nightmares.

I did a quick internet search and sure enough clear calcite promotes relaxation, aids sleep and encourages positive dreams!

This (for obvious reasons) really triggered something positive in me and led me to start researching the benefits of different crystals for both my family and my own wellness. My knowledge has gradually started to grow and I have been using crystals most days with positive results, especially when it comes to settling racing thoughts at bedtime!

My lovely sister bought me an excellent book called *Crystal Companion* for Christmas and it gave me the nudge I needed.

So I wrote down on that "2020 – I'm going to take it easy" bucket list that I would like to do some crystal healing training, so that's exactly what I have done.

I completed an online course and exam and was proud to achieve a Level 3 Diploma in Crystal Healing. It is fascinating stuff; the powerful combination of learning and crystals really did give me a boost of confidence and now I use crystals during Reiki therapy.

There are many different types of crystal, all formed differently depending on the mineral they are made from and the conditions in which they grow. It takes millions of years for crystals to form underground. Due to the way they are formed, it is believed by many (including me) that they have the ability to hold different energies and have healing properties, that can rebalance the body, mind and spirit, hence why they are used in healing therapies such as Reiki.

I am not going to give you a crystal lesson right now but as I find all crystals soothing in some way, I wanted to share with you a few of the favourites I love to work with (they can also be found in my coat pockets, at the bottom of my handbag, around the laundry room floor or in the washing machine).

Rose quartz aka 'the loving stone' is a powerful healing crystal, promoting love, self-love, friendship, deep inner healing and feelings of peace and improving sleep quality. My rose quartz always sits on my bedside table (or at least it does when the three-year-old has not pinched it).

Clear calcite (aka Iceland spar – which makes me chuckle as I always imagine a UK supermarket merger) – this is the stone that my five-year-old picked out (little did he know then that it encourages positive dreams). I use this calcite when the negative thoughts go into overdrive. During the day I carry it on my person; at bedtime I will pop it under my pillow. I also have a yellow calcite which is a great energy booster, especially if feeling run down.

Amethyst is such a beautiful purple stone, great for balancing the emotions (and my hormones). I will pull this one out when feeling irritable or stressed out for no good reason. I will hold it in the palm of my hands until I feel calmer.

Labradorite is the stone that captured my attention when I was studying for the diploma. It is believed to be a stone of magic, great for healers and anyone exploring spirituality. A perfect choice for those on a journey of self-discovery (I was certainly on one of those when it jumped out at me). It is also great for relieving headaches. Another one I carry around with me.

Black obsidian is the stone I reach for if I feel I (or my client) needs protection from a negative person or negative energy. It can help release resentment, fear and anger, especially when those emotions have been projected on to us by someone else. Running my tumbled stone through my fingers is very soothing.

Learning something new is so good for your wellbeing, self-belief and confidence, and when your subject is about something so positive and magical as crystals it even delivers you extra tools for Your Wellness Toolbox.

Crystals have been magical for my wellness in recent months, can they bring a little magic to yours?

Effectiveness: 9/10. I love working with crystals and find them very effective to soothe my nerves and racing mind, especially at bedtime.

Ease: 7/10. Now I have done the research and have a collection of crystals I find it easy to use them. However, some effort will be required to do a little research and source the crystals that are right for you. That said, crystals do tend to choose you, so next time you are in a shop that is selling crystals, go and pick out the ones that you are immediately drawn to and just watch how relevant your choice will be for you.

Cost: £0.75 – £ depends. I have bought small tumbled crystals for less than £1, yet some of my larger rough crystals have cost over £15 each. It all depends on type, size, quality and your budget. Just a warning: when you start buying crystals, you may not be able to stop!!

HOSPITAL APPOINTMENTS & VISITS

My fear of hospitals resulted in a number of panic and anxiety attacks over the years, some before I even reached the main entrance. If I did make it through the door, as soon as the hospital atmosphere hit me, the panic would start to kick in and I would bolt to the nearest bathroom. It made no difference if I was visiting a loved one or attending an appointment, the fear was the same and very real.

I know I am not alone. The fear of hospitals is very common and for many different and understandable reasons.

It was during my first pregnancy in 2014 that I realised it was time I had to face the fear as I would be making multiple trips over the coming months for all things bump related, and these special appointments should be filled with excitement, not dread.

I got proactive and signed up for Tool #24 – Hypnobirthing. I knew when I signed up that hypnobirthing would arm me with a number of relaxation tools to help me throughout pregnancy, the birth and in the early days of motherhood. Yet I was gobsmacked when after the first session my fear of hospitals appeared to have disappeared. A few days later I went for a scheduled blood test and it wasn't until I had been sat in the waiting room for a million hours that I realised at no point had I thought/worried/panicked about this appointment. I hadn't even 'subconsciously' brought along Tool #1 – Water… What had happened? I had released my fear just by talking about it honestly and openly in a positive forum? No way?!

I haven't looked back but I never take anything for granted and so these are tools that I may still call upon today when heading to the hospital:

TOOL #1 WATER

No further explanation required.

TOOL #2 BREATHE

You should be getting the hang of this one by now.

TOOL #3 MUSIC

Whether en route to see a loved one or whilst waiting patiently for your appointment, the positive playlist can come in great use as a distraction tool to drown out any negative thinking.

TOOL #8 RESCUE REMEDY

If you are starting to feel anxious about the hospital visit, then a quick spray or a few drops of Rescue Remedy in your bottle of water can help to keep you calm.

TOOL #10 ACCEPTANCE

This is a tough tool to use and ironically 'accept' at times, especially if your hospital trip is to visit a loved one who is extremely unwell or if your own appointment is to receive some potentially life-changing test results.

If you are able to 'accept' that what is happening is not something you can control and that the negative thoughts will not change the outcome, it may not make the outcome any easier to accept but it may help you approach a difficult hospital visit more calmly and with a more positive outlook. It may even help you handle the more difficult emotions more easily, like anger and frustration.

For me, I have now 'accepted' that hospitals are places where extremely sad things have happened in my life and I can't change that; I have to stop focusing on the bad things that have happened and focus on the many positive and wonderful things that have happened under the hospital roof. Friends and family have recovered well after serious illnesses, I have also received excellent care, and lots of lovely babies have been born in the hospital that used to scare me the most, including my lovely two.

TOOL #12 NO

It is not always possible to say 'no' to a scheduled hospital appointment, but if the timing clashes with other important and/or stressful life events that may result in extra stress and therefore panic, then contact the hospital and try and rearrange to a date and time that will enable you to deal with it more positively. This is also making use of Tool #9 – Daily Self-Care.

If you have been asked to visit a loved one in hospital at a challenging time for you and you have said 'yes' because you feel guilty if you don't, yet it is causing you stress and panic, then take a step back; work out if you can say 'no'. If you can (e.g. they have other visitors) then take a big gulp and say 'no'... and then maybe visit at a time that will be more positive for all.

... And if you are at the receiving end of emotional blackmail (we all know what illness can do when someone is bored) then pull this tool out with force and set some boundaries!! Easier said than done but when you've done it once you will do it again.

TOOL #15 GRATITUDE

In your diary write a gratitude note against hospital appointment dates. For example:

"I am grateful for the NHS care I am receiving and the good results I will receive."

On the morning of an appointment wake up and say 'thank you' for three positive things that will happen that day. Start the day positive and it will be harder for the negativity to get through.

On your gratitude vision board (Tool #7) stick up a picture of your loved one who is in hospital and be grateful for the care they are receiving. Be grateful for the hospital. Be positive about the hospital. I know this is not easy to do but it can help.

In the past few years one of my VIPs has had quite a few 'short breaks' in hospital and I have been the primary visitor. I know that replacing the feeling of fear with the feelings of gratitude towards the actual hospital has made all those visits so much easier and in more recent years, I can honestly say, anxiety free.

Although admittedly my tools are still overworked when the hospital visit involves A&E!! Working on it!!

… And finally, if you have a deep-rooted fear of hospitals it may be useful to explore Tool #6 – Cognitive Behavioural Therapy (or alike) as you may be able to get to the root cause and overcome it for good!

Talking Tools Blog: Originally published October 2018

TOOL #35
TEACHING OTHERS

Thomas, my five-year-old (at the time), was unexpectedly off school one day when I had an appointment with the nurse for a B12 injection. I also had to go for blood tests at the local hospital. I was unable to arrange childcare, so he came along with me.

This was October 2019, I was fast-approaching rock bottom once more and I was extremely anxious at the thought of going to the appointments, heightened by the fact I was trying so hard to hide it from him. I was retching before we left, physically shaky and tearful, so as soon as we got in the car the positive playlist was turned on and turned up. It helped. As did the breathing exercises, Rescue Remedy and positive affirmations as we approached the surgery.

However, it was another tool that I was to acknowledge at that visit that was to completely dissolve the feelings of anxiety before I even reached the nurse's room.

Whilst we sat in the waiting room, Thomas randomly asked me if I could teach him how to tie his shoelaces. Of course I agreed. As we sat there engrossed in this activity, giggling together at his first attempts, concentrating on each effort and celebrating his successes I got completely lost in the moment. I lived in the moment. I completely stopped worrying about what was about to happen, or whatever I was worrying about, and I actually enjoyed that moment in that moment.

It was not until I left the surgery that I acknowledged that I felt OK, so we then went to look at the fish and birds in a nearby pet store and on the way home I took a detour, a little trip down memory lane, to show Thomas where I used to live when I was his age. As I continued to teach Thomas in those moments I forgot about the anxiety, I didn't feel stressed; it turned out to be quite a special day.

I realise 'teaching others' has been a tool I have unknowingly had for a while. It has helped me refocus, increased my confidence and improved my communication skills. I just had not stopped to appreciate it as a tool. The shoelace lesson allowed me to do just that.

For over 18 months I have been a Your Wellness Toolbox coach, coaching others how to discover and fill their very own wellness toolboxes. I love it. It is very rewarding to see others discover their toolboxes full of tools to overcome their challenges and blockers, and then achieve their goals. As part of the coaching process I naturally teach others about my tools to encourage them to think about their tools. It always gives me a buzz and puts a smile on my face when I witness them conquer their fears, meet their goals and more importantly acknowledge how amazing they are. Again, I had not stopped until now to appreciate that this is the 'teaching' tool.

I have learned so much when teaching others. It has also helped me grow.

Effectiveness: 8/10. When I acknowledge it, teaching others has really helped me and boosted my own confidence.

Ease: 7/10. It depends if you are trying to home-school your six- and three-year-olds in the Covid-19 lockdown!!!

Cost: It costs nothing to teach others (in fact you may even be paid to use this tool).

"In teaching others, we teach ourselves."

(Proverb)

THE SCHOOL GATES
(OR SIMILAR 'GATES')

Today I went shopping for school uniform. The joys! My eldest officially starts 'real' school next week. He will walk his little, yet forever growing, feet (that will no doubt require three new pairs of shoes by the end of term) through the school gates and into reception class. The gulp in my throat as I handed over the credit card was not just about the cost…

As he shares his youthful excitement, I do my utmost best to join him on this exciting journey of discovery and utmost best (and beyond) to avoid sharing my anxieties. The irrational and the rational ones. The completely selfless mummy ones and the completely selfish (we can be) mummy ones.

The school gates can be an emotional rollercoaster and

an extremely intimidating entrance for a four-year-old. The big people feel it too.

I joined said gates last year when our boy entered nursery at the very same gates. I can't forget the nerves and nausea I felt that day; there were a lot of busy butterflies that day and urges to bolt. As he grabbed hold of me the last thing I wanted to do was let him go. My Wellness Toolbox was working overtime for both of us. These are the tools that helped me then and I know will be in full force next week:

TOOL #1 WATER

If you are taking on the nerves of all family members, keep a bottle by your side and take a few sips if you feel the nerves kicking in.

TOOL #2 BREATHE

In for five. Out for ten. If you sense or know your child is feeling nervous about their first day then you can do this together. Let them count and for just a few minutes distract them from any worries they may be having.

TOOL #3 MUSIC

My four-year-old loves to have a 'getting ready' party (shortest party ever – no wine or gin involved – so please don't be disappointed). Turn the positive playlist on and turn getting ready for school into a 'getting ready by the end of the song' moment of fun.

The song in the car on the way to school will be our boy's choice, keep his mind focused on something fun. Then when I climb back in the car after drop-off and those held-back tears start falling (guaranteed), the uplifting positive playlist will be called upon once more.

TOOL #4 NO MEDIA

Turn the news and social media off before school. Do not let the rest of the world get to you or your children on such an important day for you.

TOOL #5 ESSENTIAL OILS

If you like to diffuse oils, then this is the recipe for any school day. It is called liquid sunshine for a reason:

- 3 drops of grapefruit
- 3 drops of lavender
- 2 drops of orange
- 2 drops of peppermint

TOOL #14 POSITIVE PEOPLE

Try and ignore (hard I know) any school gate politics that exist (it amazes me that such a thing does exist). Be the positive person that smiles and acknowledges everyone (no matter how annoyed you still are at how hard it is for a child to put a sock on). Every parent at the gates had a journey that morning. If someone ignores you it may just be because they have had the worst morning ever trying to get their child(ren) to school or they are just as anxious as you. Or they may just be a complete '&%$£', so just be grateful you have dodged a bullet!!

TOOL #15 GRATITUDE

As we take the route to the school gates, I will say 'thank you' for at least three things I am grateful for:

- Thank you for the beautiful views we see on this journey.
- Thank you for all the new things my son will learn today.
- Thank you for all the positive people who we will meet and support us on this journey.

TOOL #16 LET GO & RELEASE TECHNIQUES

I know that the best thing I can do for our son is to let go and let him grow. I can't let my fears and anxieties of this 'big bad world' hold him back. If the anxiety starts to take over, I will call upon the 'pebbles' for a few chats. I may even grab the matches or light the fire and WIDABI – write my fears, anxieties or worries down, burn them and let them go, so when I reach those school gates, I have released some of the anxieties and fears, so I don't pass them on to my child or others.

TOOL #20 LEARN SOMETHING NEW

Your child is going to, so why don't you?

TOOL #25 WRITING

Write this moment down in your journal or diary. Your child may be excited, scared, worried, happy, sad... or all the above. Write this memory down to release or to share. Let your child know how proud you were on this day.

Talking Tools Blog: Originally published September 2018

YOUR WONDERFUL
WORLD ALPHABET

During the Covid-19 lockdown when I attempted to home-school, I found this activity in one of the packs provided by the school. It caught my attention as it reminded me of the Positive Shopping Basket game my sister and I invented (we like to think) on a long car journey last year.

I completed the activity with my son, realised the benefits and now it is something I encourage my loved ones and clients to do.

Just thinking of the things you love in your world (people, places, hobbies, any of your favourite things) can be good for your mind, can make you smile and encourages you to recall happy memories.

This can be a useful tool to put the brakes on an overthinking mind in overdrive or just for fun – a great game to play on long car journeys (and causes less arguments than Yellow Car).

All you have to do is write down or say out loud the wonderful things in your world for each letter of the alphabet. Do it alone, with friends or as a family.

A

B

C

D

E

F

G

H

I

J

K

L

M

N

O

P

Q

R

S

T

U

V

W

X

Y

Z

TOOL #36
DRAWING

In March 2020, just days before the UK was told to self-isolate due to Covid-19, I was fortunate enough to spend the weekend with a lovely group of Tool #15 – Positive People at a wellness retreat with *Breathe Retreats*. This was a 40th birthday gift to myself, a weekend to fully charge Tool #9 – Daily Self-Care, meet like-minded and friendly faces, devour healthy and nutritional food, partake in yoga (even though it gives me nausea) and pilates (I found this more enjoyable than I thought I would), sit in a hot tub with a glass of fizz (my kind of retreat), learn about new wellness tools and of course add some of them to My Wellness Toolbox.

On arrival we were welcomed with a beautiful gift bag full of wellness-related gifts, including a motivational pad and tin of pencils. It did make a couple of us chuckle that the quote on the front of my pad was 'Creativity is Contagious, Pass It On'... quite ironic considering what was happening in the world at that time!

There was a very good reason for the pad and pencils, one that would have quite a profound and long-term impact on me.

During one of the sessions we were set a simple challenge to find a quiet spot inside or outside and create something with our new tools. I decided to grab a chair, I moved it in front of a window, the sun shone in, warming my skin, and I started to draw an owl (that was an actual ornament, Snowy wasn't perched on a tree outside) and I got completely lost in the experience. Over 70 minutes later the page was full, my hands were smudged with pencil lead, I had created something to be proud of, and more importantly I was relaxed. So relaxed. I had not felt that at ease or relaxed since April 2019 when we were on holiday abroad. This was so good for me. It would become even more powerful for me within weeks.

Just days later we would find ourselves self-isolating, quickly followed by the Covid-19 lockdown. All schools and nurseries to be closed for the foreseeable; the assumption by many is that children will not return to school until September 2020. As I sit here writing this it is April 2020; for three weeks I have been 'trying my best' to home-school my five-year-old and keep my three-year-old off the tablet for more hours than she is on it. Life has changed dramatically for us all, routines are out the window, so many unknowns, and we fear what Covid-19 may do to us or our loved ones if we catch it. Anxiety has been doing its best to take over once more. Tools are flying and one of the more effective ones for me and the children has been that pad of paper and lovely tin of pencils.

Each day during lockdown we have Art Hour. The first day it was just for the children; I switched on Tool #3 – Music, the positive playlist, and laid out paper, colouring books, pencils and pens, so whilst the five-year-old got creative and the three-year-old vandalised the woodwork, it gave me a chance to catch up on some of 'my jobs'. Yet on the second day I had an urge to join them; instead of 'my jobs' I put on some classical piano music (that had been introduced to me on the above retreat by a lovely lady called Jag) and I grabbed my pad and pencils. We agreed to draw something we could see in the room; I chose a Buddha ornament (that I bought at Buddha's birthplace when we travelled in Nepal) and once again got completely lost in creation. It makes me feel so calm. I just focus on what I am creating. Any worries simply disappear for that hour.

There is a reason that children love drawing and colouring: they know how good it is for them.

Drawing or colouring may not be for you. Not everyone on the retreat wanted to use the pad and pencils; instead they went to explore outside and got creative with their cameras, taking photos of the nature around us – just as relaxing.

Getting creative not only relaxes you. It can improve your memory, helps you release negative emotions, reduces anxiety, improves concentration, makes you happier, and the more you create, the more creative you become. Those that are more creative often look for simpler and more effective ways of solving issues and making things work.

So, grab your pens, pencils, paints, sewing kit, wooden spoon, camera… and create something. Add them as tools to Your Wellness Toolbox and keep them charged.

Effectiveness: 10/10. Every time I use this tool I always feel better for it.

Ease: 8/10. Finding the time isn't always going to be easy. During lockdown Art Hour has become part of our routine; when lockdown is lifted, I really want to continue using this tool on a regular basis, yet I am realistic that time could be a constraint. I need to remember that when I use the tool it has got to be one of the easiest and most enjoyable to use.

Cost: Free – £depends… it all depends on how creative you want to get.

EXAM TIME

This week one of my lovely Reiki clients got in touch to arrange for me to work with her teenage daughter who is currently taking important exams; the nerves have kicked in, anxiety is rapidly taking over and emotions are heightened. These are common feelings for all ages when preparing, revising for and taking any kind of exam. Therefore, as exam season is fast approaching it didn't take two seconds to decide what scenario to tool you up with this week. Exams.

My A-level exams were over 20 years ago (ouch!) but I still remember those nerves, the butterflies dancing around my knees and brain, the nausea and the desire to run. My choice to then progress in the IT industry and my desire to constantly learn new things meant that exams were never going to be a thing in my educational past but very much a part of my professional future.

In more recent years My Wellness Toolbox has come to effective use to help me manage and overcome the nerves and stress during the build-up to, and on, exam day. As I look down the list of my 26 tools, I reckon most them have probably been used in some way, so at the risk of rewriting My Wellness Toolbox I have picked out my top ten wellness tools for exams:

TOOL #1 WATER

When revising make sure you keep yourself hydrated as it is a proven fact that this can improve both memory and concentration. However, water to me is not just about hydration; without failure I will take a bottle of water with me into any exam. When feeling nervous, sipping water can help relax you and can even prevent an anxiety attack. This tool costs very little, yet can prove very valuable when the nerves kick in.

TOOL #2 BREATHE

If during revision or when taking the actual exam, you start to feel overwhelmed, take a step back and breathe. This is the breathing exercise that brings me a sense of calm very quickly and can help clear the clouds and reset the mind. Practise it daily and it will be even more effective.

Breathe in for five. Breathe out for ten.

- Make sure your feet are on the ground
- Try and breathe in through your nose and out through your mouth
- Take a deep breath in and count to five
- Take a deep breath out and count to ten

It does not matter how quickly you count or for how long you do this exercise, just repeat this until you feel calmer.

TOOL #3 MUSIC

Music may be a distraction whilst revising, however when the books have been closed for the day turn the music on, turn it up and reset your mind.

Create a positive playlist packed with the songs that lift you. On the day of the exam, wake up (if you managed to sleep), turn the music on, turn it up.

En route to your exam try and avoid cramming last-minute information into your already busy mind; instead listen to the positive playlist, it can help you remain focused.

… And when you walk out of the exam and your head is buzzing, turn the music on and up, let your mind switch off. It deserves it.

TOOL #5 ESSENTIAL OILS

There are so many essential oils that can help you through exam time, including:

- Rosemary – perfect for concentration and improving memory
- Peppermint – keeps you focused and alert
- Sweet orange – uplifting and mood-boosting

When revising get the diffuser going. On exam day, if you are unable to use essential oils (with a carrier oil) on your skin, you can put a few drops on a hanky for you to have a sniff of during the exam.

TOOL #8 RESCUE REMEDY

A drop of Rescue Remedy in your water whilst revising, or to sip on before or during the exam, will help you remain calm or resettle you if you do start to feel nervous or anxious. Sometimes just having it available to you will put you at ease. Bach for kids is also available.

TOOL #9 DAILY SELF-CARE

When you are so busy with your head in the books it is easy to forget to have some downtime and make it 'me' time. When planning your revision make sure you schedule in time for a break, a walk, a relaxing bath, listen to your favourite music... do nothing!! Anything that you will enjoy that also allows your mind to reset.

After each exam, say 'thank you' to yourself for all the hard work you are putting in, and don't forget to give yourself a little reward.

TOOL #11 AFFIRMATIONS

Take five minutes to think of positive affirmations that you can refer to in moments of doubt. Write them down, stick them to a wall or somewhere you will see them every day; most importantly say them out loud every day, several times a day. A few examples:

- I feel clear, calm and confident for my exams.
- I will stay focused and pass exams easily.
- I will be relaxed during my exams.
- I can recall information easily and quickly.
- I will nail it!!

TOOL #12 NO

Even if it feels like it sometimes, the exams do not last forever, yet the reason you are taking exams may be for your forever plans, therefore they are very important to you. Learn to say 'no' to yourself, and others, when the distractions or the demands come along that could impact on your time to revise or put unnecessary pressure on you during exam time.

TOOL #15 GRATITUDE

Use the Gratitude Tool with force during exam time. Being grateful about the opportunities to learn and develop and for all of those around that support you during this time can make your experience more positive; this can have a direct impact on your results.

When you wake up:

- I am thankful for all the new things I will learn today.

When revising, at the end of each session write/type on your notes:

- Thank you for all the valuable information I will retain for the exam.

In your diary write a big 'thank you' against the important exam days:

- Thank you, I nailed it today!!

TOOL #26 ME (THAT'S YOU!)

Don't forget the most important tool. You! Look after yourself and keep yourself charged.

Good luck!

Talking Tools Blog: Originally published May 2018

TOOL #37
DECLUTTERING

One Sunday afternoon in January I pulled out Tool #9 – Daily Self-Care and Tool #16 – Let Go & Release Techniques and took myself on a decluttering mission.

Three bedrooms down and lots of great clothes, bags, other random 'stuff' and even a baby monitor (I did not know we owned) to donate to the charity shop. There goes Tool #21 – Kindness flying by once more.

It was also amazing what I found, including a precious necklace I thought I had lost over a year ago; I had tears of joy when I found it 'in a safe place'.

Decluttering 'stuff' also helps declutter the mind and can be really good for your wellbeing. It is making space for new and positive things to come into your life.

... And at the bottom of our wardrobe I found *the* 'anxiety boots'.

Just before I hit rock bottom in 2006 I was desperate for an answer. As I searched the internet I came across a book that guaranteed it would remove my anxiety within weeks, and if within 28 days I wasn't "cured" I could claim a "no quibble refund". It cost £130!!!

This is not the kind of money I had to spend on a book, yet I was anxious, tired, vulnerable and desperate, so I bought it on my credit card. It arrived a few days later.

It was heavy, it was thick, it was detailed, it was complicated... it was scientific... it made me more anxious! I decided to go to the hassle of returning it and fortunately I did get my money back. At the point I received my refund I had already paid the credit card bill. I had also hit rock bottom which had led to me sitting in the Cognitive Behavioural Therapy (Tool #6) chair, so was starting to feel a little more confident. I decided to take that £130 'bonus money' and treat myself to something lovely to make me feel good; I chose some lovely new leather boots.

When I found them tucked away in the bottom of the wardrobe, I realised I had not actually worn them for over ten years as the toes curled up and they need repairing, but they have always reminded me of how well I did at that time. How even in bad times I made some good decisions. How I did not let that anxiety beat me. I have not let them go for those reasons. They have moved house with me seven times!

However, I questioned why I was holding on to them. Yes they remind me of how well I did, but they also represent the past. It was time to let them go.

... And make space for some new shiny boots (because I haven't got enough pairs already!!!!).

I actually closed one eye as I pushed them into the charity bag and wondered if I should just get them repaired as they really are lovely boots. This may sound ridiculous to some of you reading this, but this was a big step to boot them out (excuse the pun!) as they represent a huge achievement in my life. I felt a little emotional. Then I felt a huge sense of relief; it was as if I had finally let go of that period in my life that no longer serves me. About bloody time!!

It is said that "more mess means more stress", therefore "less mess means less stress". Decluttering can decrease anxiety levels, increase your ability to focus and can even improve sleep.

What are you holding on to from your past and why? Is it time to declutter?

Effectiveness: 8/10. A good declutter can make you feel 'lighter', yet it can also remind you of everything else that needs decluttering. Walk into it with an open mind and accept it is an ongoing process.

Ease: 6/10. Where do you start? That is the hardest part. Then finding the motivation. 54321. Then the time? Yet when you work all that out and start to declutter it can be enjoyable, especially when you find old treasures and happy memories.

Cost: This one can make you money!!! Not everything has to go in a charity bag, there are several buy-and-sell sites you can choose from to sell your preloved items and make some money... to buy some new loved items.

YOUR POSITIVE PEOPLE

"Surround yourself with positive people who will support you during your bad days, not just your good days."

(Unknown)

Every choice we make is influenced by the people in our lives. So, when choosing the tools for Your Wellness Toolbox, I highly recommend you grasp your Positive People Tool with both hands and make them essential.

When you surround yourself with positive people it not only makes you happier and can improve your health and wellbeing, but it also makes you far more aware of those who are not a positive influence in your life. You can then make the choice to stand back from those who don't enrich and support you and spend time with those who want to help you grow.

Think about what a positive person looks like for you.

For me, positive people are friendly, warm, easy to talk with, trustworthy, supportive of the decisions I make, able to share and celebrate both our successes, honest with me, compassionate, encouraging, energetic and fun to be with. They bring out the best in me.

… And someone who is not a positive person?

A person that is not a positive influence in my life focuses on the negative, may make me feel anxious in their company, make me feel drained after spending time with them, criticises my character, judges me and talks negatively about me and others, displays jealousy and does not support or celebrate my growth.

Can you easily identify the positive people in your life?

This may feel a little brutal, especially if like me you try and see the positive in everyone, yet when I did this honestly and used my 'gut feelings' this exercise really helped me focus my time and energy on the supporters in my life and that was the best thing I could do for my own wellbeing.

- Paper and pen required
- Make a list of between five and 20 people you spend the most time with
- Next to each name put either a '+' or a '−'
- Put '+' if you enjoy their company and look forward to spending time with them. You feel good when in their company and you mostly feel loved and supported by them.

- Put '–' if they make you worry, feel stressed or anxious in their company. You do not look forward to spending time with them; when you do it feels like they suck out your energy, make you feel less or upset you.
- Now, using your gut feelings, put a score from -5 to +5 to rate how much of an effect they have on you. You are not rating the person, you are rating how you feel when you spend time with them.
- You now have a list that indicates who your positive people are.
- Go spend time with them

TOOL #38
PLACENTA ENCAPSULATION

"My name is Ali Swift and I had my placenta encapsulated."

There I wrote it. Out loud. Done. In print.

… And for a known reason I did not share this with you in *My Wellness Toolbox*. That reason? I feared your judgement. Placenta encapsulation brings with it a dollop of controversy and a splash of mixed opinions. Some friends rolled their eyes and quite harshly threw their judgement at me; sadly I allowed that to rule and at the time of writing *My Wellness Toolbox* I obviously had not let that go and made the conscious decision to not include this extremely effective tool.

Thankfully that has been something I've continued to work on in the past few years, i.e. letting go of the fear of judgement by others and being confident in my own decisions. So, now I am sharing it with you. In fact, now I feel a sense of guilt for not sharing it sooner.

Deciding to encapsulate my placenta following the birth of our daughter was one of the best choices we made during our second pregnancy. For us it was an incredible tool for my mind and my body, had a positive impact on the whole family, and, like Tool #24 – Hypnobirthing, I used it proactively for several health benefits.

Why placenta encapsulation?

The placenta is full of nutrients and hormones that benefit both mother and baby throughout three trimesters of pregnancy, therefore some mothers choose to have the placenta turned into capsules to consume for the fourth trimester (i.e. when the baby is born), as it is believed to bring a number of health benefits, including a quicker recovery following the birth, increased milk supply, reduction in postnatal bleeding, reduction in the risk of baby blues, therefore also minimising risk of postnatal depression. Also, a great source of iron and other important vitamins. I was one of those mothers.

A few months after my first was born I started to experience anxiety, triggered by overthinking and intrusive thoughts. I had moments of paranoia and was convinced I must be experiencing postnatal depression. I knew what to do and headed straight to my GP. He once again asked me to talk through how I had been feeling and really listened. He took everything in and said, "Ali, I think you are a tired new mummy who needs to try and find a way to get more sleep." He then asked me to go for blood tests that day. Within 24 hours it was confirmed I had a B12 deficiency and I was prescribed some B12 supplements. Within two weeks I felt 'normal' again, had more energy, was sleeping more easily (when baby – and husband – allowed) and the anxiety significantly reduced.

Therefore during my second pregnancy, when chatting to my hypnobirthing specialist and miracle worker Liz Stanford (The Calm Birth School), who knew about my experiences (and also lack of milk supply with my first born), she suggested I explore placenta encapsulation, as it may just ease some of the fears or worries I was starting to have because of past experiences. It really did help; just putting a plan in place to do this made me feel better.

The placenta encapsulation process that we chose involved taking the placenta, steaming, dehydrating and grinding it, and placing it into capsules to be taken as pills. This was all done by a placenta remedy specialist, Victoria Webb (After Birth). The look on my husband's face when he thought he may have to get actively involved still makes me laugh out loud today.

My placenta was steamed and infused with lemon, ginger and chilli – which always makes me smile as I love anything with these 'warming' ingredients. According to traditional Chinese medicine it is believed that the body is left cold after birth and therefore needs warming, so these help towards rebalancing.

Victoria also used my placenta to make an ointment that I used effectively to treat my daughter's nappy rash and my eczema which often flares due to raging hormones. I also have a placenta tincture that will last a lifetime. I can use it when required to treat PMS symptoms (I guess my husband will be a good person to comment on its effectiveness) and it may even be beneficial for my emotional wellbeing when I face the menopause. I turned down a placenta smoothie; I don't think I could have faced that straight after birth.

So, two days after our beautiful daughter was born by C-section, Victoria delivered the placenta capsules to our door and I started to take them straight away. Within a matter of days I was bouncing around the house, my husband had started calling me Dairy Crest due to the fantastic flow of milk (and I was expressing only), my scar healed very quickly, I felt very balanced and was able to return to sleep as easily as the baby following night feeds. I felt good and energised. In the words of my husband: "Pass me those pills."

The placenta pills really did make a positive difference for me and my baby. That is why I would encourage anyone who is pregnant to explore this as an option, no matter how squeamish the thought may make you. It could really help your mind, body and emotions at such a special time in your life.

I was once sharing my placenta encapsulation success story and someone listening in suggested: "Oh, I don't believe in any of that, must have been a placebo effect." My response:

1. "I am so grateful that I am open to try new things that could support my wellbeing. I respect not everyone is."
2. "Well, it worked for me"

If you have a tool that worked for you but you have held back sharing it with others for fear of judgement, pull out Tool #16 and try to 'let it go', as sharing it may just have a positive impact on someone else's wellbeing too.

Effectiveness: 10/10. Extremely effective for me. My husband was gutted he couldn't have popped the placenta pills.

Ease: 7/10. This tool may come with opinions and judgement from others which may discourage you from using it. This will also require some research, which, depending on stage of pregnancy, may feel like effort. Victoria (After Birth) was recommended to me which made the steps of finding a local placenta remedy specialist a lot easier. When you do find the right specialist for you the rest is straightforward as they do the hard work for you. Oh, apart from the giving birth bit; that will require some effort from you.

Cost: £150 – £400. It really does depend on the process and package you choose. We paid £250.

YOUR DREAMS & GOALS

Let's do some simple goal-setting for *you*.

Goal-setting can be daunting and when you are feeling negative about moving forward in any area of your life to achieve your dreams it can feel impossible.

However, when we write down our simple goals that are realistic it can really help boost our mood, confidence and overall self-belief when we achieve them.

This is a simple brainstorming exercise to help you set goals for any area of your life, including work, home, finances, relationships, health, to help you focus on *you*!

You will need your journal/notepad/piece of paper and a pen.

Oh, I love a good brainstorm.

Part 1. Create a similar brainstorm diagram to below

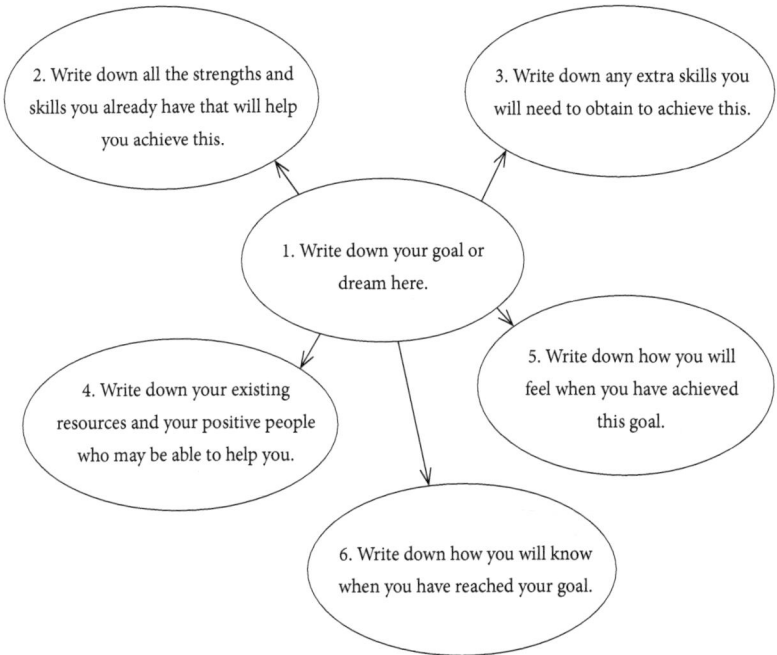

2. Write down all the strengths and skills you already have that will help you achieve this.

3. Write down any extra skills you will need to obtain to achieve this.

1. Write down your goal or dream here.

4. Write down your existing resources and your positive people who may be able to help you.

5. Write down how you will feel when you have achieved this goal.

6. Write down how you will know when you have reached your goal.

Part 2. Small steps

Now, think about the next three (or more if you wish) small steps you can take towards achieving this goal.

Next to the step put a date by which you would like to take that step.

Remember, do not put any pressure on yourself, make sure timescales are realistic.

	Step detail	Due Date:
Step 1		
Step 2		
Step 3		

Check in with yourself every day/week/month (delete as appropriate) to see how you are progressing. Keep the steps updated with progress and completion dates.

Repeat Part 2 until all the required steps have been taken to meet your goal.

Part 3. Celebrate your achievements

When you have reached your goals and your dreams have become reality make sure you write down your wins, congratulate yourself and celebrate with the positive people in your life.

A real-life example:

Crystal healing is something I had thought about learning about for a while. Crystal healing would not only support my wellness but would also be great for my Reiki clients. I just needed to pull my finger out. So, when writing down my 2020 goals I made sure "Learn more about crystal healing and gain a qualification" was included and this is how I put it in motion:

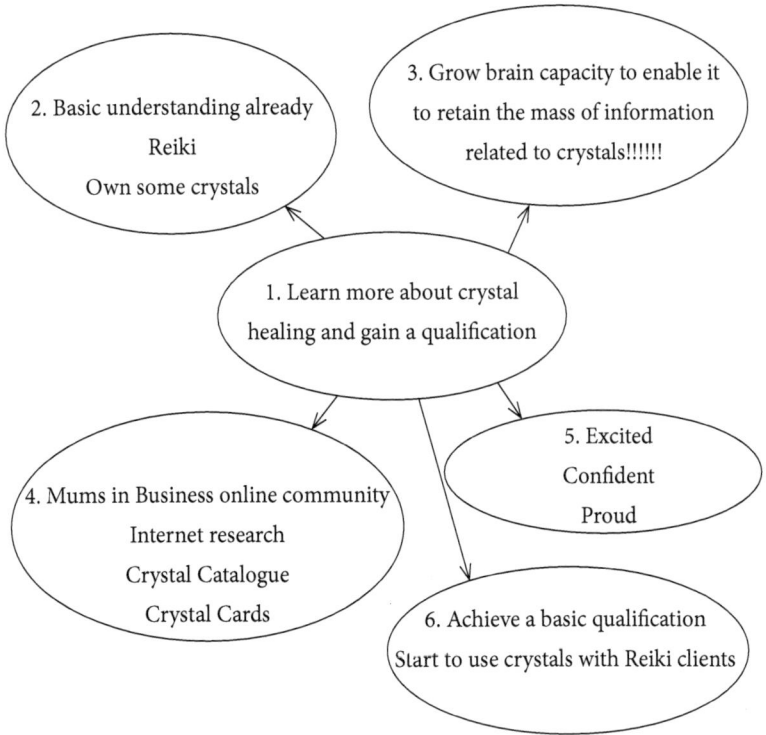

2. Basic understanding already
Reiki
Own some crystals

3. Grow brain capacity to enable it to retain the mass of information related to crystals!!!!!!

1. Learn more about crystal healing and gain a qualification

4. Mums in Business online community
Internet research
Crystal Catalogue
Crystal Cards

5. Excited
Confident
Proud

6. Achieve a basic qualification
Start to use crystals with Reiki clients

	Step detail	Due Date:
Step 1	Start to read crystal book and use crystal cards received for Christmas	New Year's Eve (31 December 2019) Completed
Step 2	Reach out to the Mums in Business Association via Facebook and seek guidance about courses – online or face to face?	New Year's Eve (31 December 2019) Completed
Step 3	Research costs and book online course	7 January 2020 (Completed 2 January)

I repeated Part 2 and continued to add and take the required steps. They were small, realistic and did not overwhelm me. I successfully completed an online course and achieved a Crystal Healing Diploma... and it did not feel hard.

"Life is happening for you, not to you."
(*Work Your Light* – Rebecca Campbell)

TOOL #39
FORGIVENESS

Woah! This one has got to come with a warning. It is a tough tool to use. Yet when you can learn to use it, this tool can reduce anxiety and depression and can bring you peace of mind, enabling you to move forward more positively.

It was only when I was sat back in the talking therapy chair in December 2019 that it became evident there were still some past events, some traumatic, others less so, that I had not forgiven myself or others for. There was still some leftover anger and hurt festering inside, slowly releasing itself, quite painfully, as anxiety.

I thought I had successfully used Tool #10 – Acceptance and Tool #16 – Let Go & Release Techniques. There is no denying they had helped, yet there was definitely more effort required for the deep-rooted stuff. Cue the arrival of Tool #39 – Forgiveness for some extra support.

Definition of Forgiveness (Cambridge Dictionary)

Forgive (verb); to stop blaming or being angry with someone for something that person has done, or not punish them for something

When we pull out and use this tool we make a conscious effort to release the feelings of anger or resentment we may have towards someone (or ourselves – I'll come back to this one shortly) because of something they have done, regardless if we actually agree they deserve it.

It does not mean we have to paper over the cracks, condone their behaviour; it does not mean you have to 'patch things up' if there has been a fall-out, or forget about what has happened. Forgiveness enables you to find peace in a situation, to let go of the anger. Using the Let Go & Release Techniques has helped me with this, especially WIDABI (Write It Down And Burn It).

In that talking therapy chair I was able to forgive people and situations that have happened without having a conversation with anyone other than my therapist. So much resentment and anger released; it even makes me feel more positive about some of the individuals, some of whom do not even realise the hurt they caused. It has also given me a new perspective on the events and why they happened, really supporting my 2020 mantra, "This is happening for you, not to you." All of this forgiving did result in Tool #28 – Crying making quite a few appearances, also helping me release and heal. Powerful stuff.

Then there is the matter of forgiving yourself. Also known as self-forgiveness. This can be so hard to do yet one of the most important and rewarding things you can do for your wellbeing and life. If we do not use this tool, we get stuck in the past and prevent ourselves from embracing the present.

It is human nature to feel guilty about past mistakes; we have all made them, some of them may be shockers, we may be waiting for others to forgive us before we forgive ourselves. Yet holding on to those mistakes, waiting for others' forgiveness (that may never come), allowing that guilt to contaminate us, using the self-sabotage stick to beat ourselves up, will not benefit us or others in any way. In fact it may lead to more self-sabotage and even more mistakes.

Turns out I have been feeling subconsciously guilty for a very long time, about something that was actually not my fault. That guilt had slowly eaten away at the flesh of my self-esteem over decades. Those outdated beliefs pop up once more. Turns out I did not do anything wrong; I had no reason to forgive myself. I just need to forgive myself for beating myself up over something I had not done. Or do I? Maybe I just need to give myself a break and be kind to my mind.

It takes time but when you combine those three power tools, Acceptance, Let Go and Release Techniques and Forgiveness, amazing and positive things will happen for you.

Effectiveness: 10/10. Yup. This one is a game changer.

Ease: 4/10. Forgiveness is not always an easy tool to use, as you may not even realise you need to pull this tool out. It was only by talking to a trained professional, establishing the triggers for the anxiety I was experiencing again and working through past events that I was able to acknowledge that I did need to use this tool for my own wellbeing. I'm extremely grateful I did; as I said above, it has been a game changer.

Cost: Forgive for free

"Holding on to resentment is like drinking the poison
and expecting the other person to die."

(Buddha)

A GLOBAL PANDEMIC

At the start of May 2020, a large retail group approached me to share some of the tools in My Wellness Toolbox with their employees. The teams are unable to work in-store due to the government-enforced lockdown, however at some point they face another wave of change, especially when the high street reopens and they can step back into their old routines that may look significantly different.

This was produced to encourage the teams to prepare for that next wave rather than worry about it, and for them to start thinking about and proactively using the tools that may help them flow more positively through those waves of change.

THE TOOLS NAVIGATING ME THROUGH THE LOCKDOWN WAVES (8 May 2020)

It has been just over six weeks since the UK went into lockdown and many of us were forced to stay at home for all the right reasons, bringing a new way of life behind closed doors.

New routines, new roles (including some around the waist for me), new habits. Less travel, less socialising, less certainty. We were forced to adjust. Some of us found it easy, some of us found it difficult, some of us are still trying to work it out, some of us are resisting it. I am sometimes all the above on the same day. That is why the tools in My Wellness Toolbox are being used with force right now to help me live in the moment.

I am also aware that this is not 'forever'; further change is ahead of us. When lockdown is lifted, we will be given permission to step back into our 'normal' life and pick back up old routines, although they may look quite different. Some of us are excited by this and can't wait for it to happen, some of us are daunted by it and fear more unpredictable change. I swing between both. That is why the tools in My Wellness Toolbox will also be used proactively with force to ensure I am prepared when the change comes.

These are just a few of the tools that have helped me reduce the overwhelming feelings, remove the guilt of living behind closed doors whilst friends and family go out on the frontline and that encourage me to live in the moment and to think more positively.

TOOL #4 MEDIA – TURN IT OFF

If you are watching, scrolling, or reading anything in the media and it does not make you feel good then switch it off.

When we are feeling overwhelmed, anxious or stressed, watching an upsetting storyline on our favourite soap, reading about crime in the local newspaper or scrolling through a mass of friends' opinions on social media can trigger the stress response, making us feel even worse.

Think about the information you are allowing your mind to absorb; it will make a difference to how you handle today and tomorrow. If you have a choice, try to make it a positive one for your mind.

If you want to switch something on, make it your positive playlist or your peaceful playlist. Music is another endorphin-pumping tool that can help uplift or relax you when you need it most.

TOOL #16 LET GO & RELEASE TECHNIQUES

I have several techniques and tools I use to help me let go of worries and stress. I know the importance of releasing my negative emotions and thoughts. When I keep things trapped inside, my mental health declines, my stresses increase. If we do not release our worries now, they will be forced out at a later date, maybe without warning.

- **Write**: Writing helps clear the mind. Grab a journal and put down how you are feeling in words. If you are feeling negative this is a great way to get it off your chest; you can then choose to burn it and watch the worries burn away. I call this WIDABI – Write It Down And Burn It.

If you are feeling good, then write down all those positive thoughts. Then if you do stumble across a bad day you can pick up your journal and your own words may lift you.

- **Talk:** Talking and being open about your feelings is one of the best ways to cope with a worry or problem that is overplaying in your head.

  When we share with others, it not only makes us feel less alone, your words may just help the person you are talking with, encouraging them to also open up and let go.

  Do not feel that your worries or concerns are less important than someone else's. We are all different; we all have different life experiences, different levels of resilience and tolerance, different strengths. We are all in different boats, yet the same storm right now. All of us trying to navigate our way through. If we talk, we can help and guide each other, making the journey less stormy.

- **Cry:** We enter the world waving this tool in the air, letting the world know we have arrived, yet many of us grow up thinking that crying is a sign of weakness. It is not. Crying is an important self-soothing tool; it activates the parasympathetic nervous system enabling your body to calm down.

  Crying releases endorphins including oxytocin; these are feel-good chemicals that can help relieve both emotional and physical pain.

Tears also detox the body; emotional tears contain stress hormones and when we cry, we are flushing them away. Releasing tears during a time like now is very important to help your mind process and accept what is happening.

TOOL #2 BREATHE

The great thing about this wellness tool is that it can be used any time, anywhere and it doesn't cost a bean. Breathing exercises can stop anxiety and panic attacks in their tracks, instantly reduce stress, and can even help you sleep. I have also recently discovered they are essential when trying to home-school a six- and three-year-old!!

There are many different breathing exercises to try; this is the one that works best for me:

Breathe in for five. Breathe out for ten.

This takes a little practice but once mastered you will be using this exercise with little effort. It is very effective in making you feel calm very quickly in different scenarios.

Try it now.

- Make sure your feet are on the ground
- Try and breathe in through your nose and out through your mouth
- Take a deep breath in and count to five
- Take a deep breath out and count to ten

It does not matter how quickly you count or for how long you do this exercise, just repeat it until you feel calmer.

Breathing exercises are also a great way to start or end the day. Just breathe. Just be.

You can use all these tools on the good, the bad and the ugly days. Allow them to support you as we continue to adjust through the coming weeks and months.

GRIEVING

Use your tools.
In your own time.
In your own way.

TOOL #40
YOU (THAT'S ME!)

Tool #26 in My Wellness Toolbox is ME (that's YOU!). This is the tool that keeps all the other tools charged.

Yet since *My Wellness Toolbox* was published, I have really appreciated how much you and Your Wellness Toolboxes have also kept my tools charged, especially when I have taken your tools and added them to My Wellness Toolbox.

Please never underestimate how important you are for yourself and others, or how important others are for you.

Please keep talking, sharing and charging Your Wellness Toolbox. I will keep talking tools and sharing My Wellness Toolbox.

When you find the value in yourself your whole world will change.

Thank you.

"I am enough."

_____

_____

_____

_____

_____

_____

_____

_____

_____

_____

_____

_____

_____

_____

_____

_____

_____

_____

_____

_____

_____

ALSO BY ALI SWIFT

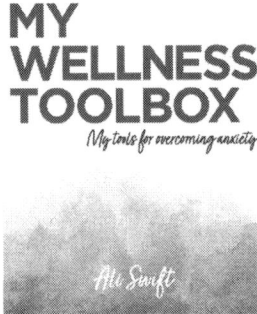

**MY
WELLNESS
TOOLBOX**
My tools for overcoming anxiety

Ali Swift

"My Wellness Toolbox by Ali Swift is, without a doubt
the best self-help book that has been written and
published in the past couple of decades"
That's Books – Press Review

You can find out more about Ali Swift and the services she
provides, including Your Wellness Toolbox 121 Coaching
and Your Workplace Wellness Workshops on the website:

www.aliswift.co.uk

Follow Ali Swift and My Wellness Toolbox on Social Media

www.facebook.com/AliSwiftUK
www.instagram.com/AliSwiftUK
www.twitter.com/AliSwiftUK